STEPHEN OWOLABI

BEYOND THE BUZZ

A YOUNG MIND'S GUIDE TO SEX AND SELF-WORTH

BEYOND THE BUZZ

A Young Mind's Guide to Sex and Self-Worth

Stephen Owolabi

DEDICATION

This book is dedicated to all young minds across the globe.

CONTENTS

INTRODUCTION

Life often brings us to a crossroads. Behind us lie our memories, past choices, and experiences that have shaped who we are today. Ahead of us stretches an endless path, influenced by the decisions we will make. Here's the reality: every choice we make impacts our lives, but some choices carry far greater weight and have the power to shape our entire future.

As a young adult, life can feel like a whirlwind—relationships, peer pressure, and the desperate desire for acceptance can be overwhelming. Social media, movies, and even our friends often paint a picture that suggests the only way to fit in is to go along with the crowd, even when their choices may lead us down a harmful path.

At this stage, it may seem like your goals, values, or beliefs don't matter. It can feel like the world demands you to conform, even when that isn't the path you envision for yourself. Sometimes, exposure to sex happens early, often before one fully understands its implications. But deep down, is this truly what you want for the life God has given you?

What if you could step back and choose a path that is entirely your own? What if you prioritized the person you are becoming over the pressure to conform? What if purity wasn't about rules imposed on you but a choice that brings strength, confidence, and clarity?

Mary Ellen Ashcroft, in her book *Temptations Women Face*, shares the story of a young girl named Sammie:

Sammie is a ten-year-old girl who lives around the corner from us. She brags about the R-rated movies she watches when her father passes out drunk. She dyes her hair blonde and dresses to show off her developing body. When my thirteen-year-old son is around, she sits provocatively on our front steps, talking to my seven-year-old daughter, telling her how cute her older brother is.

Sammie's story is not unique. Society today exposes children to harmful influences at an alarming rate. The rise of juvenile delinquency and early sexual activity among young people is a growing crisis. What makes it worse is that many of these influences are disguised as entertainment or education. A child who can read and write can easily access explicit content, sex-positive messaging, and ideologies that normalize premature sexual experiences. Shockingly, these influences often go unchecked by parents, educators, or society at large.

In many cases, the very people young people look to for guidance—parents, media, and community leaders—fail to offer the direction they need. Some parents, due to their own negative experiences, discourage their children from choosing purity, believing it to be futile. As a result, instead of focusing on education, skills, and personal development, many young people are steered toward distractions that can lead to regrettable consequences.

Scripture teaches that everything has its time. Engaging in sexual activity prematurely can place the mind, body, and future at risk. The stakes are high when it comes to premarital sex, and the consequences are often more severe than anticipated.

At just ten years old, Sammie is already burdened by pressures no child should face. With an absent, alcoholic father and a distorted view of self-worth, she seeks validation through attention-seeking behaviors. But the real question is:

Does Sammie truly understand what she is doing, or is she simply reacting to the pressures surrounding her?

In a journal I once read, a young woman commented: *"Why all the fuss about avoiding premarital sex? I'm a virgin, but I find these conversations uncomfortable. If two people love each other, what's the harm?"*

Her perspective is not uncommon. Many young people, influenced by peer pressure and modern narratives, believe that love and sex are inseparable. Scientific studies have even endorsed sexual activity for young people as early as sixteen, with some arguing that waiting until eighteen is unnecessary.

Reading her words, it was clear that she had internalized these societal messages. She was simply waiting for the right moment—when she fell in love—to let things take their course. But where did she learn that love must equate to sex?

For many, the youthful years are a time of passion and adventure. However, when that passion is misdirected toward sex and reckless behavior, the consequences can be devastating. The damage to one's emotional well-being, future goals, and personal identity can be immense.

But here's the truth: **You are not Sammie.**

You have a bright future ahead of you, filled with potential and purpose. You don't have to follow a confused crowd or compromise your worth just to fit into a society that distorts love, attraction, and identity. **You are priceless, and you deserve more than the baggage that comes with reckless choices.**

This book is here to help you discover your unique voice, chart your own course, and make decisions that align with your future and authentic self. The coming chapters will guide you in embracing a life of purpose, confidence, and clarity—one where you choose a path that truly reflects who you are meant to be.

CHAPTER ONE

IT'S NOT JUST ABOUT SAYING "NO"

The first misconception about purity is the mindset that says "no is a restriction that stops you from living your best life."

Have you ever stared back at yourself in the mirror and asked, "Who the hell am I?" or, "What am I supposed to be doing with my life?" The profound answers to these questions will serve as a guide to search yourself and, most importantly, bring you to terms with what you stand for.

Understanding yourself first is critical because when it comes to sexual purity, knowing who you are and who you will become can make all the difference.

Sexual purity isn't just the ideology of not having sex till after marriage; it's so much more than you can exhaustively put into words. It is a reality, a mindset, and a choice that screams, "I have so much respect for myself. I value my body above everyone else. I know my worth and I choose to do only what represents the respect I hold for myself. Hence, I will only do what is best for me and my future."

Exactly How Powerful Is Purity?

To be very honest, the urge to do things that will cause everyone to like us can be overwhelming—especially if you are a people pleaser. Most times we watch people flaunt their pictures or relationships, and even rub their sexual activities in our faces if they are quite close to us.

Let's face it; these things get to us a lot of times and make us feel like acting like everyone else is necessary to fit in. But when purity is taken in its full length, breadth, depth, and height, it offers us a way out of the pressure that we might otherwise feel—distracting us from our true purpose.

You can wear a cool smile and make it known that you don't need to do what everyone else wants to do to feel valuable. You can proclaim how powerful your standards make you feel and how much control you have over yourself. The ability to stay pure unashamedly can be really empowering—if we let ourselves see this reality.

Not everyone can be you, and that is profoundly powerful and refreshing.

The Bible clearly states that we should not conform to these pressures and standards influenced by immorality and filth. Romans 12:2 says, "Do not conform to the pattern of this world, but be transformed by the renewing of your mind. Then you will be able to test and approve what God's will is—his good, pleasing and perfect will."

When we choose purity, we consciously choose to see ourselves in a different dimension and decide the kind of lives we want to live. Choosing purity is our way of declaring that God's plans for us will always beat temporary attractions and a lush lifestyle.

The Wiser Choice

Purity is not just the power of saying no; rather, it is the choice of saying yes.

Choosing purity is saying a bold yes to a future without the inhibition of blemishes, a yes to a mental dynamite mindset, to sound health, self-respect, and to a life that is free of regrets and pain.

2

Choosing to stay away from premarital sex symbolizes the hope we hold for a perfect future, the beauty of our purpose in life, as well as the strength of our will to stay true to ourselves.

Each time you turn down an invitation to premarital sex, you strengthen the boundaries that ensure your safety. Just like the guardrails on steep mountain trails, these boundaries ensure you stay on the safe path, follow the right course on your journey, and protect you from tripping and falling into fatal grounds.

Put simply; every day you decide to stay sexually pure is the day you add a new layer of protection to your heart, your mind, and, in effect, your future.

Our Present Choices, Our Future Realities – How Do They Go Together?

Every single action we carry out in life either draws us closer to our dreamed future or pulls us farther away from those expectations. Our teenage years and young adulthood are not stages to be careless about because they represent our most fertile season as human beings. This is a season to dream big, plan out our goals, and begin to sow quality seeds for our future. But most times, the greatest distractions—such as early involvement in sexual intercourse—can confuse us, blur our visions, and derail progress by focusing our young minds away from the big picture.

Every good thing we achieve in life begins with an idea born out of a thought or dream, but dreams without intentional actions are mere imaginations. It takes practice, discipline, and intentional efforts to bring our dreams to reality. The Bible in Proverbs 29:18 clearly highlights this fact: "Where there is no vision, the people perish." Put simply, without putting in the time, effort, and discipline that your future requires, it's very easy to be overwhelmed and get lost in pleasures that will rob you of your long-term blessings and fulfillment. How do you make sure that you're doing the right thing, which your future self will be proud of as a teenager or young adult?

3

1. **Ensuring That You're Making Wise Investments in Your Daily Decisions**

    Let's look at it this way: your time, focus, and efforts are currency. What you use these three things to purchase today will determine the things you'll own tomorrow.

    Two paths and two choices are before you – (a) you either invest your time, energy, and focus on careless youthful escapades, teenage drama, fights over girls/boys and relationships, crying over heartbreaks (the list is endless); or (b) you invest your time, energy, and resources in self-discovery, achieving excellence in academics, acquiring skills that will set you up for future success in any industry of your choice, staying fit and healthy by engaging in exciting sports, building your spiritual soundness, leading in interesting social clubs, traveling to explore new experiences, and basically building the future you look forward to.

    The question is, is it going to be A or B? You can't have both and you can't live twice. You only live once, as they always say. But what are you going to live for? There's a cheat code though: you can have B first, and when you've achieved your goals, you can settle down with your desired partner and have all the sex you want for the rest of your life. I bet you're wondering if it can work the other way around. Haha! The truth is, IT CAN'T. Just as you say A before Z, and not Z before A, sacrifice takes the stage. Sacrifice means giving up something important for the sake of other considerations that lead to a better-planned future. This is you taking the driver's seat instead of allowing peer pressure or the environment to dictate what your future should be.

    What's the summary of all that we are saying? It's simple! Your youthfulness is for smashing goals, not for chasing people. God gave you that energy as a youth to build the life you want to enjoy when you're older. For everything, there is a season and a time for every matter under heaven (Ecclesiastes 3:1). While the earth remains, seedtime and harvest, day and night, cold and heat, winter and summer shall not cease (Gen 8:22). This means that the same law that binds the seasons of winter and summer, day and night, heat and cold, is the same law that ensures every man will receive the results of his actions in due time (seed time and harvest). So, if you don't have to pray for day and night to occur, then be rest assured that your harvest is coming based on what you sowed. It's a natural law, programmed to ensure that the circle of life is not cheated. Once again, I ask you, what kind of investments are you making for your future? What kind of future will you have judging from your current choices?

Consider a young woman who dreams of becoming a doctor. By staying focused on her studies and avoiding the distractions of an unhealthy relationship, she graduates with honors and achieves her lifelong ambition. Contrast this with a peer who became entangled in a toxic relationship, leading to emotional burnout, a drop in grades, and an unfulfilled dream.

2. **Banking on Delayed Gratification**

In general terms, delayed gratification can be defined as the power to resist temporary desires and temptations in favor of long-term rewards. This is the lifestyle of successful people. The Bible further justifies this in Galatians 6:9, "Let us not become weary in doing good, for at the proper time we will reap a harvest if we do not give up."

Delaying sexual activities gives you the space to pursue other activities that are aligned with your purpose in life—provided you have taken an interest in discovering what that purpose might be. If you ask most young people today what their purpose in life is, many would probably be clueless, and for some it might not be a priority because they still have time to figure it out. While that might not be entirely wrong, remember that a journey of a hundred years starts in a single day. Therefore, taking seriously how you would like the trajectory of your life to go early on will prevent you from misdirecting your energy when it is abundant. Delaying emotional relationships until you are more mature and have learned the ropes to building a successful relationship makes a difference. In the meantime, you allow yourself to focus on developing your skills, discovering your purpose, and building strong character. It's about saying "no" to immediate gratification so you can say "yes" to a brighter future.

Life Story: Simone Biles is an Olympic gold medalist today who chose to prioritize her training and career goals over entanglements during her formative years. Her dedication paid off, as she is now one of the most celebrated athletes of this generation. Her story is one of the simplest illustrations of the power of focus and the rewards of delayed gratification.

Again, our ultimate example of all time, Jesus Christ, endured the cross for the prize that was set before Him. Hebrews 12:2 states, "Looking unto Jesus, the author and finisher of our faith; who for the joy that was set before him endured the cross, despising the shame, and is set down at the right hand of the throne of God." Jesus Christ encourages us to hold fast to our godly faith and endurance. God does not abandon us when we pass through temptations or suffer. "Blessed are those who suffer for righteousness' sake, for theirs is the kingdom of Heaven" (Matt. 5:10).

3. **Never Forgetting That Sexual Entanglements Can Distract Us from Our Dreams**

Early sexual relationships come with relationship issues, drama, heartbreak, and confusion that often cloud our judgment and disrupt our priorities. Relationships are not a taboo, but the baggage that accompanies them can be a child's worst nightmare. This is why it is better to fully abstain from these relationships and build positive friendships instead—until you are a grown adult who has your life together and is ready to settle down in marriage. This way, you prepare yourself for wholesome, safe, and rewarding relationships rather than toxic ones.

Involvement in early sexual relationships sometimes creates unhealthy bonds that are hard to break, forcing young people to remain in toxic situations they shouldn't be in because of fear. Corinthians 6:18 warns us to "flee from sexual immorality. All other sins a person commits are outside the body, but whoever sins sexually, sins against their own body."

4. **Laying the Bricks for a Healthy Future Free from Collateral Damage**

Staying focused does not imply that you shouldn't keep friends or interact with people; rather, it means doing so with wisdom. This approach helps fuel your dreams instead of hindering them with mistakes. Consider the following steps:

a) Write down your goals. Research shows that when a goal is written down, the chances of achieving it are higher, as it serves as a personal check and a daily reminder of who you are and what you're living for.
b) Create necessary boundaries. Ensure that you protect your energy, time, and resources from time wasters and distractions.
c) Do not associate with people you don't want to be like. Make sure your friends and companions positively influence your goals. Proverbs

13:20 says, "Walk with the wise and become wise, for a companion of fools suffers harm."

d) Have an accountability partner—a respectable mentor, friend, or family member who motivates you to stay on track.

In the Bible, Joseph is a prime example of someone who kept his dreams in focus despite immense challenges. Sold into slavery and falsely accused, Joseph never wavered from his vision. His dedication and faithfulness eventually led to him becoming the second most powerful man in Egypt, fulfilling the dreams God had placed in his heart (Genesis 37–41).

Susan was a young entrepreneur who dreamed of starting her own business in the tech industry. After becoming involved in a toxic relationship, she quickly snapped out of it and decided to postpone dating to focus on her career. After channeling her energy into her passion for about six years, she launched a successful company by her mid-twenties. She later entered a healthy, mature relationship with someone who supported her vision, proving that dreams and love can coexist when pursued in the right order.

5. **Ensuring That Your Faith Remains Intact While Pursuing Your Goals**

Without faith, it is impossible to even believe in the possibility of your future. The ability to trust God and His timing gives you the strength to say no to relationships that don't align with His purpose for you. Jeremiah 29:11 reminds us, "For I know the plans I have for you," declares the Lord, "plans to prosper you and not to harm you, plans to give you hope and a future." No matter how smart, strong, or wealthy you may be, never stop praying over your dreams and future to gain clarity, peace, and discernment on what to do and what not to do.

In conclusion, sexual purity is a profoundly powerful declaration of faith and self-respect. It paves the way for a life of fulfillment, focus, and discipline by keeping God at the center of your life. Remember Philippians 4:13, "I can do all things through Christ who strengthens me."

Your dreams are worth the sacrifice. By aligning your choices with your goals and trusting in God's plan, you can build a future that reflects His glory. Remember, every decision you make today is a step toward the person you're becoming tomorrow. Choose wisely, dream boldly, and trust God every step of the way.

CHAPTER TWO

TARGETING INFERIORITY COMPLEX: RECOGNIZING IT, OVERCOMING IT, AND EMBRACING A LIFE WITH PURPOSE

What is an Inferiority Complex?

Inferiority complex is the result of a constant feeling of not being enough (inadequacy), which often leads to unhealthy compensatory acts. These actions can show up as timidity, withdrawal, overcompensation, or even aggression. For instance, some children often bully other school children because they feel a sense of low self-esteem and seek to feel better by being mean (a display of dominance). This is one way to see that a child is mirroring their silent battles in toxic ways—this is their coping mechanism.

Children who come from physically or psychologically challenging backgrounds mostly try to hide their secret struggles by looking for recognition or validation from unthinkable places or through unwise actions. An old childhood acquaintance, whom I'll call Edwards to keep him anonymous, is a perfect example of this concept. He was very charismatic and intelligent. He grew up dealing with emotional scars that pushed him into assuming that being a great hunter of girls was the key to exercising dominance. If any girl proved hard to get, that would be his next target, and he would have countless sexual partners. The attention he got from other guys during his lame games was a means for him to seek validation, but the result was escalated conflicts and painful consequences he wasn't prepared for. All the girls fought for the sorry crown and wanted to keep him, so they struggled to gain the most attention from him.

This is not any different from the way teenagers and youth get involved in the act of sex. Hence, some, in their bid to gain prominence within a clique, would fight it out through sex—bringing the high and the mighty down to their bed—without knowing that this way leads to the grave (Prov. 7:21-27).

Edwards was one of the many examples we have in society today that portrays how an untended inferiority complex or deep-seated insecurities can be a quick vehicle to devastating disasters.

Self-Worth and Behaviors

The way we see ourselves greatly influences how we relate to people around us. A lot of young adults today constantly struggle for approval and validation from everyone else but themselves, and at some point, they make grave decisions that reflect their low self-esteem.

The problem is, it doesn't stop at telling lies to feel secure or bullying the next kid to feel better. They go further into the worst kinds of sexual relationships to fit into circles, jeopardizing their spiritual and emotional well-being—forgetting who they were made to be in the first place.

Remembering what we are made of is one profound way to avoid such pitfalls in life. The Bible clearly tells us how God made us:

"You made all the delicate, inner parts of my body and knit me together in my mother's womb. Thank you for making me so wonderfully complex! Your workmanship is marvelous and how well I know it. You watched me as I was being formed in utter seclusion, as I was woven together in the dark of the womb. You saw me before I was born. Every day is recorded in your book. Every moment was laid out before a single day had passed. How precious are your thoughts about me, O God! They are innumerable! I can't even count them; they outnumber the grains of sand! And when I wake up in the morning, you are still with me!" — Psalm 139:13-18 (NLT)

If you are the kind who looks for outside validation to know your worth, take this to heart. The Psalmist took a moment to focus on all the complex mechanisms that make the functioning of his being possible and concluded that he was fearfully and wonderfully made. From this point, you should recognize that whatsoever opinion others have of you is unimportant because the one who made all the curves around your body made you beautiful, and you therefore do not need validation from those wishing you destruction. A lack of love and reassurance from parents, especially, can be detrimental; but for someone who recognizes that the One who made them invested so much thought in every strand of their being, you have no need to be bothered by what people think of you.

It is usually said that if you have children and do not show them love, someone else (who does not truly love them) will come with a sugar-coated tongue, speak to them sweetly, and lure them away to abuse them. They will easily fall victim because even though you love them as your children, sweet words and pretense (especially when a parent isn't intentional enough) will make a child fall prey to a wolf in sheep's clothing.

Children from broken homes or two-parent homes lacking stability and support are oftentimes the most vulnerable to the ills present in their homes or in society in general. Compared to homes where the parents have a strong sense of commitment to themselves and the love they share, single-parent homes are sometimes an open breeding ground for cultivating low self-esteem. In other cases, some parents stick together but are violent and exchange all sorts of abusive language at home. These actions produce negative influences on their own children. Children then turn elsewhere for the love and affection which they desperately desire and deserve, without evaluating from which persons such affections are coming—whether it be someone who wants to take advantage of them (usually of the opposite sex), peer pressure, or some sexual pervert who, in the name of showing them love, begins to abuse and expose them sexually.

God is not ignorant of this, and that was why He spoke through the Psalmist concerning us:

"For you formed my inward parts; you covered me in my mother's womb." All who claim me as their God will come, for I have made them for my glory. It was I who created them. (Is. 43:7)

Keep in mind that the love of God is not fleeting but constant and intentional. God's love is the best news for children who have inherited traumatic effects from their environments. He says,

"For I know the plans I have for you," declares the Lord, "plans to prosper you and not to harm you, plans to give you hope and a future." (Jer. 29:11) You've probably not realized that God filled every part of you intentionally and created you with His own essence so that He can show forth His glory through you. He is not like some earthly parents who don't care about your welfare or how you feel. He intentionally (not mistakenly) fitted your body together beautifully (you are fearfully and wonderfully made) for only His glory.

Have you ever looked at yourself in the mirror and realized how perfect you are? Do you ever pause amidst your busy schedule to say, "God, I see that You made me so beautifully and full of Your glory. Thank You for making me with so much love and grace"? Take a moment every now and then to appreciate how He has done a wonderful work in bringing forth a unique you. The beauty or handsomeness that He gave you is so that you can glorify Him with it.

I urge you to never forget that God is in control even when it seems your life is falling apart and the pressures around you are overwhelming. Be comforted in His word and understand that whatever challenges may arise—anything that might make you doubt God's love for you—are meant to be stepping stones to the next level of your life journey. Don't ever give up on yourself because God would never give up on you.

The story of Sarah in Genesis 12:14-20 and Genesis 20:2-4 tells us of the power of self-worth and faithfulness in God. Sarah maintained her dignity despite trials. Despite being placed in compromising situations, Sarah upheld her integrity and glorified God with her beauty and character. Here's the background of the story: when they arrived in Egypt, everyone spoke of Sarah's beauty. Even the palace officials sang her praises to their king, Pharaoh, and she was taken into his harem. Abraham told people there that his wife, Sarah, was his sister.

Impressed, Pharaoh gave Abram many gifts because of her—sheep, cattle, donkeys, male and female servants, and camels. But the Lord sent a terrible plague upon Pharaoh's household because of Sarah, Abram's wife. King Abimelech sent for her and had her brought to him at his palace. Then one night God came to Abimelech in a dream and told him, "You are a dead man, for that woman you took is married." But Abimelech had not slept with her yet, so he said, "Lord, will You kill an innocent man?" (Gen. 20:2-4) Consequently, Pharaoh's household called for Abram and accused him sharply because of what had happened: "What have you done to me? Why didn't you tell me she was your wife? Why were you willing to let me marry her, saying she was your sister? Here is your wife! Take her and be gone!" Pharaoh then sent them out of the country under armed escort—Abram and his wife, with all their household and belongings. (Gen. 12:14-20)

Now, do you know that Sarah was 65 years of age when the servants of Pharaoh took her to be given in marriage to Pharaoh? Abraham had put this beautiful woman in a tight corner to make her commit adultery by telling the Egyptians that she was his sister, not his wife. There is something worthy of note in that incident.

God communicated His mightiness to Pharaoh and his kingdom because a woman served God wholeheartedly in all humility, even though she was beautiful. What was paramount in her heart was to seek to please the One who gave her the beauty—she knew He gave it to her so she could reflect His glory. At this point, the Bible had not yet told us that Abraham had become rich. He ran to Egypt to get food and survive. What do you think the environment of Pharaoh's palace would look like to Sarah, bearing in mind that Pharaoh was one of the greatest kings in the world at that time? Think of the serene and clean environment she would move into. Think of the servants and maids who would be at her beck and call. Yet she would not allow that to crush the image of God in her—that image of being fearfully and wonderfully made. She did not see herself as inferior to the king because the One who gave her the beauty would also give her the throne at the right time.

You are a young person, and if someone you see with some clout around town, who has been intimidating your neighbor, calls you to bed, think about what your reply would be.

Lessons From Sarah's Story

1. **Like Sarah, we must recognize our worth as a reflection of God's glory.** Our outward beauty and inner strength should align with (and not oppose) His purpose for us.

2. **Your physical and emotional well-being are gifts from God.** Preserving them requires intentionality.

3. **True beauty beyond artificial make-up.** While external enhancements can accentuate appearance, true beauty is nurtured through inner peace, good health, and confidence in God's design.

4. **Align always with God's plans for us.** By honoring God's purpose for your life, you ensure your actions and decisions reflect His glory.

5. **Avoid situations that devalue or undermine your worth.** Never misuse your gifts or allow others to exploit them; God gave them to you for a divine purpose.

6. **Read and meditate on Psalm 139 and Jeremiah 29:11,** understanding that you were created for a reason.

7. **"Guard your heart with all diligence because out of it are the issues of life."**

8. **Surround yourself with positive influences** and seek God's guidance in challenging times.

By understanding your unique design and embracing God's love, you can overcome feelings of inferiority and live a purposeful life. Trust in His plans, and He will lead you toward a fulfilling and meaningful existence.

CHAPTER THREE

GIVING GOLD TO THE SWINE – THE TRUE COST OF COMPROMISE

There are certain treasures of immeasurable value that we hold and must always hold onto, such as integrity, purity, self-worth, and vision. These treasures are so priceless that losing them can potentially ruin our entire existence on earth. However, little things happen here and there that cause us to compromise, and compromise is usually disguised as just a tiny act of trying to fit in—a decision that doesn't seem that harmful or something we refer to as "a small sacrifice." But the problem with these seemingly tiny "sacrifices" is that their consequences are grave and destructive. Each time we trade our pride, dignity, or values for mere fleeting moments, it is a foolish act of giving away the "gold" in our lives to the "swine" (those who offer little approval and only momentary pleasures).

A. How Do We Consciously or Unconsciously "Give Gold to the Swine"?

The term "giving gold to the swine" is derived from the book of Matthew 7:6: "Do not give what is holy to the dogs; nor cast your pearls before swine, lest they trample them under their feet, and turn and tear you in pieces."

According to the context, swine represent those leeches around us who are not worth losing something precious to. Gold, on the other hand, represents our wisdom, virginity or bodies, identities, dreams, and so on. Compromising these "golds" often results in us losing ourselves—a loss of dignity, brokenness, and deep regret.

When we compromise on our principles, it usually does not seem like we are doing something major; rather, it sneaks up on us in little, seemingly harmless choices—like flirting with colleagues, a casual exchange of kisses here and there, paying for an exam because you're not feeling up to it, and basically trying to please people by ignoring your personal values.

In Genesis 25:29–34, we see how Esau trades his rightful place and inheritance for a bowl of food. His hunger blinded him, causing him to give up something priceless for his immediate satisfaction. Just like Esau, sacrificing your purity can leave you feeling robbed once the excitement fades, having given away something of immeasurable value for a foolish reason.

1. How Expensive Is Compromise?

a) Emotional Costs

• **Regret** – When you can't undo what you've done to yourself, you must live with the regret for the rest of your life. Nothing can change the past.

• **Guilt** – Acting against what you know in your heart leaves a gnawing sense of guilt that lingers in your gut.

• **Broken Relationships** – Compromise can erode trust and respect in relationships, potentially ruining the future that could have been.

b) Physical Costs

- **Loss of Opportunities:** Poor choices can derail your future goals, whether academic, professional, or personal.

- **Loss of Sound Health:** A significant percentage of incurable diseases today stem from wrong choices and relationships, such as HIV/AIDS, high blood pressure, heart attacks, STIs, depression—the list goes on.

- **Diminished Self-Worth:** Giving away what is precious can make you feel unworthy and disconnected from your God-given identity.

c) Spiritual Costs

- **Distance from God:** Compromise often leads to sin, which separates us from God. Isaiah 59:2 reminds us, "But your iniquities have separated you from your God; your sins have hidden His face from you."

- **Missed Blessings:** God calls us to obedience not to restrict us, but to position us for His best. Compromise takes us out of alignment with His will.

2. Society's Role in Encouraging Compromise

In today's world, society often downplays the consequences of compromise. The media glorifies instant gratification, relationships devoid of commitment, and success achieved at any cost. Social media portrays lifestyles and relationships that are often unattainable or fake, pressuring young people to conform. However, this pursuit often leads to comparing oneself to others and making poor choices simply to fit in.

Example from Modern Culture: Celebrities or influencers may glamorize behaviors such as casual relationships or excessive partying, but the behind-the-scenes stories of brokenness and struggles often remain untold.

3. Protecting Your Gold – Practical Steps to Resist Compromise

To avoid the trap of giving what is valuable to the swine of compromise, here are practical ways to stay grounded in your values:

1. **Know Your Worth**

   Understand that you are a child of God, created with purpose and value. Psalm 139:14 declares, "I praise You because I am fearfully and wonderfully made; Your works are wonderful, I know that full well."

2. **Set Clear Boundaries**

   Write down your personal and spiritual values. Establish clear boundaries for relationships, entertainment, and lifestyle choices. When you know where you stand, it becomes easier to say no to anything that doesn't align.

3. **Choose Accountability**

   Surround yourself with like-minded friends who share your values and will encourage you to stay on track. Seek out mentors who can guide you in wisdom and love.

4. **Focus on the Bigger Picture**

   When tempted to compromise, think about the long-term consequences. Ask yourself:

   o   Will this choice bring me closer to my goals or further away?

   o   Does this honor God and the person I want to become?

5. **Stay Connected to God**

   Regular prayer, Bible study, and worship strengthen your resolve and help you discern right from wrong. Proverbs 3:5-6 reminds us, "Trust in the Lord with all your heart and lean not on your own understanding;

in all your ways submit to Him, and He will make your paths straight." 2 Timothy 2:22 encourages us, "Flee the evil desires of youth and pursue righteousness, faith, love, and peace, along with those who call on the Lord out of a pure heart." By choosing purity, you're not missing out—you're protecting your future and the treasures God has entrusted to you.

Your purity, dreams, and identity are treasures worth protecting. Don't trade what is precious for temporary satisfaction or societal approval. Instead, recognize your value, trust God's plan, and stand firm in your convictions.

When faced with the choice between compromise and integrity, remember: the cost of compromise is always greater than its so-called reward. Choose to honor God, pursue your dreams, and guard your "gold" for the worthy life He has planned for you.

B. Sexual Effects on the Brain – Attachment, Not Love

Sex is an experience that profoundly affects how we feel, our interactions, and even the way our minds function. It is more than simply an act of touching. God created sex to be a strong connection that unites two individuals in a way that transcends their physical selves. Understanding the mechanism behind this bond enables us to appreciate why God's design for marital sex—a gift—is strictly for a couple's psychological and spiritual well-being, as well as a moral requirement.

The Hormonal Impact of Oxytocin and Dopamine

Intense substances are produced by the brain during intimacy between two people, according to the National Library of Medicine. These substances foster connection and emotional ties. Oxytocin and dopamine are two important hormones involved in this process.

1. The "Bonding Hormone" – Oxytocin

Oxytocin, known as the "bonding hormone," promotes trust, closeness, and connection. It is released in large quantities during physical contact, particularly during sexual activity, effectively serving as an emotional glue that holds two people together. In a dedicated, loving marriage, this connection is ideal and lovely. The downside is that it can also create bonds outside of marriage that impede one's ability to leave unhealthy or complicated relationships. For instance, the emotional connection oxytocin creates might make it extremely difficult to end a casual sexual relationship if one later discovers it is poisonous or incompatible. "Above all else, guard your heart, for everything you do flows from it," cautions Proverbs 4:23. Oxytocin exemplifies how a scientific truth can also be a spiritual truth. Premarital sex can lead to needless emotional entanglements if we do not protect our hearts.

2. The "Feel-Good Chemical" – Dopamine

Dopamine is the neurotransmitter responsible for rewarding pleasurable emotions. It is released when engaging in joyful activities including eating, exercising, and having sex. It can be tempting to pursue sexual closeness outside of God's purpose because dopamine makes us feel good. However, the emotional crash that follows the loss of the dopamine "high" can lead to sadness, feelings of worthlessness, and heartbreak. This can create an unhealthy cycle, such as cheating on a spouse due to an inability to let go of the past or even falling into depression after ending a toxic relationship.

"Do you not realize that your bodies are temples of the Holy Spirit, who is in you, whom you have received from God?" (1 Corinthians 6:19–20). You were purchased; you are not your own. Thus, use your body to praise God. Understanding the potent effects of dopamine should motivate us to use our bodies for purposes that glorify God rather than for fleeting pleasure.

24

Emotional Effects and Repercussions of Early Sexual Attachments.

There are various effects created by emotional ties from oxytocin and dopamine:

I. Unrealistic Expectations from an Obvious Mistake

A sexual connection can frequently be mistaken for true love, leading you to ignore warning signs or remain in harmful partnerships.

II. Heartbreak

The emotional pain of ending these relationships is greater than that of a normal breakup. Essentially, the brain experiences withdrawal from dopamine and oxytocin much like when an addiction is broken.

III. The Inability to Move On

It may become more difficult to build strong connections in subsequent relationships if sexual attachments are formed too soon. The emotional baggage from prior experiences might lead to trust issues, insecurity, or a fear of commitment.

According to Matthew 6:22–23, "The eye is the lamp of the body." Your entire body will be illuminated if your eyes are healthy; however, if your eyes are not healthy, darkness will permeate every part of your body. We run the risk of making our lives more confusing and painful when we prioritize bodily pleasure over emotional and spiritual well-being.

Useful Suggestions for Protecting Your Mental Health and Heart.

1. **Establish Clear Physical Boundaries**

    Set your emotional and physical limits in relationships and be sure to express them clearly. Being aware of your boundaries enables you to avoid potentially tempting situations or mistakes.

2. **Establish Moral and Emotional Understanding**

Prioritize developing a deep emotional bond through supportive interactions, shared values, and meaningful dialogue. This lays the groundwork for relationships that endure without the constant need for physical closeness.

3. **Ensure That You Surround Yourself with Support**

Look for mentors and friends who are as dedicated to purity as you are. Surrounding yourself with like-minded individuals helps you maintain your integrity.

4. **Renew Your Mind with Scriptures**

Frequent study of God's Word can help you remember His purpose for your life. The Bible encourages us to focus on "whatever is true, whatever is noble, whatever is right" (Philippians 4:8).

5. **Pray for Strength and Direction**

In your relationships, always ask God to help you honor Him. Prayer is an effective strategy for maintaining chastity, for the adversary is like a roaring lion seeking whom he may devour.

In conclusion, it's easy to get caught up in the moment and think that certain choices won't matter down the line. But the truth is, every choice we make has consequences. When we give in to pressures and compromise our values, we might feel a temporary thrill or excitement, but more often than not, it is followed by regret. The thrill fades, but the consequences linger.

Think of purity as protecting your future self. Imagine the person you want to be five, ten, or even fifteen years from now. How do you want to look back on the decisions you're making today? Will you be proud of them? Will you be able to say that you honored your values and protected your heart?

Give gold to the pig and see what it is likely to do with it. Of all the things God created, where do you think you fall—the last and best of His creation or something less? Remember Edward at the beginning of this book; as many girls as he saw wanted his attention, he gave it to them, made a mess of their bodies, and within a few weeks he sent them off—and that was the kind of life he lived. Why are you going out of your way to give your gold to the swine? It will only mess it up. Some people even seek to defend the swine and say, "Harry is just going through a tough time; he will change. He appreciates me and takes good care of me." The truth is, the Manufacturer has more value for your life than any man or woman you have met or will ever meet. No one will take care of you like God, so why are you not submitting to Him? Do so today, and He will fulfill His promises in your life.

CHAPTER FOUR

UNDERSTANDING YOUR TRUE WORTH BY SEEING YOURSELF THROUGH THE CREATOR'S EYES

When was the last time you paused what you were doing to truly reflect on your worth? I'm not talking about social media popularity or the number of likes and followers you have; I'm referring to your profound, unfaltering worth—a value that does not change like the weather, regardless of your current situation in life. Understand that this kind of worth is not derived from the people and connections you have; it comes from knowing who you are in the eyes of God.

Many of us have found ourselves in situations that make us question our worth, or even make it impossible to believe we are valuable. However, there are questions far more important than how we look, who we know, or how others see us. Chief among them is: **HOW DOES GOD SEE YOU?**

A. Seeing Yourself Through God's Eyes:

One of the sweetest realities about our relationship with our Father is that He sees us even in our darkest moments—He sees us fully, including our fears, strengths, dreams, flaws, and everything that the eyes of man are too limited to perceive.

1 Samuel 16:7 (ESV) – "But the Lord said to Samuel, 'Do not look at his appearance or on the height of his stature, because I have rejected him. For the Lord sees not as man sees: man looks on the outward appearance, but the Lord looks on the heart.'"

1 John 3:1 – "See what kind of love the Father has given to us, that we should be called children of God; and so we are. The reason why the world does not know us is that it did not know Him."

Ephesians 2:10 – "For we are His workmanship, created in Christ Jesus for good works, which God prepared beforehand, that we should walk in them."

1 Peter 2:9 – "But you are a chosen generation, a royal priesthood, a holy nation, a people for His own possession, that you may proclaim the excellencies of Him who called you out of darkness into His marvelous light."

Psalm 139:13-16 – "For You formed my inward parts; You knitted me together in my mother's womb. I praise You, for I am fearfully and wonderfully made. Wonderful are Your works; my soul knows it very well. My frame was not hidden from You, when I was being made in secret, intricately woven in the depths of the earth. Your eyes saw my unformed substance; in Your book were written, every one of them, the days that were formed for me, when as yet there was none of them."

Romans 5:8 – "But God shows His love for us in that while we were still sinners, Christ died for us."

Romans 8:38-39 – "For I am sure that neither death nor life, nor angels nor rulers, nor things present nor things to come, nor powers, nor height nor depth, nor anything else in all creation, will be able to separate us from the love of God in Christ Jesus our Lord."

Ephesians 1:4-5 – "Even as He chose us in Him before the foundation of the world, that we should be holy and blameless before Him. In love He predestined us for adoption to Himself as sons through Jesus Christ, according to the purpose of His will."

Matthew 5:14 – "You are the light of the world. A city set on a hill cannot be hidden."

1 Corinthians 3:16 – "Do you not know that you are God's temple and that God's Spirit dwells in you?"

Colossians 2:13-14 – "And you, who were dead in your trespasses and the uncircumcision of your flesh, God made alive together with Him, having forgiven us all our trespasses, by canceling the record of debt that stood against us with its legal demands. This He set aside, nailing it to the cross."

John 15:15 (ESV) – "No longer do I call you servants, for the servant does not know what his master is doing; but I have called you friends, for all that I have heard from My Father I have made known to you."

Galatians 4:6-7 – "And because you are sons, God has sent the Spirit of His Son into our hearts, crying, 'Abba! Father!' So you are no longer a slave, but a son, and if a son, then an heir through God."

2 Corinthians 5:21 – "For our sake He made Him to be sin who knew no sin, so that in Him we might become the righteousness of God."

Romans 8:14-15 – "For all who are led by the Spirit of God are sons of God. For you did not receive the spirit of slavery to fall back into fear, but you have received the Spirit of adoption as sons, by whom we cry, 'Abba! Father!'"

Matthew 5:13 – "You are the salt of the earth, but if salt has lost its taste, how shall its saltiness be restored? It is no longer good for anything except to be thrown out and trampled under people's feet."

Galatians 3:26-27 – "For in Christ Jesus you are all sons of God, through faith. For as many of you as were baptized into Christ have put on Christ."

Psalm 139:14 – "I praise You, for I am fearfully and wonderfully made. Wonderful are Your works; my soul knows it very well."

2 Timothy 1:7 – "For God gave us a spirit not of fear but of power and love and self-control."

Ephesians 2:19 – "So then you are no longer strangers and aliens, but you are fellow citizens with the saints and members of the household of God."

2 Corinthians 5:17-21 – "Therefore, if anyone is in Christ, he is a new creation. The old has passed away; behold, the new has come. All this is from God, who through Christ reconciled us to Himself and gave us the ministry of reconciliation; that is, in Christ God was reconciling the world to Himself, not counting their trespasses against them, and entrusting to us the message of reconciliation. Therefore, we are ambassadors for Christ, God making His appeal through us. We implore you on behalf of Christ, be reconciled to God. For our sake He made Him to be sin who knew no sin, so that in Him we might become the righteousness of God."

Romans 8:37 – "No, in all these things we are more than conquerors through Him who loved us."

Romans 5:1-2 – "Therefore, since we have been justified by faith, we have peace with God through our Lord Jesus Christ. Through Him we have also obtained access by faith into this grace in which we stand, and we rejoice in hope of the glory of God."

John 15:13 – "Greater love has no one than this, that someone lay down his life for his friends."

Psalm 147:5 – "Great is our Lord, and abundant in power; His understanding is beyond measure."

Ephesians 2:4-5 – "But God, being rich in mercy, because of the great love with which He loved us, even when we were dead in our trespasses, made us alive together with Christ—by grace you have been saved."

Ephesians 1:4 – "Even as He chose us in Him before the foundation of the world, that we should be holy and blameless before Him. In love."

Take a moment to meditate on and understand the verses above. You did not come into this world by chance; you were intentionally created, cherished, and profoundly loved by God. Let that sink in. When you fully grasp the value God has placed on you, you will realize that random societal standards or people's ideas of worth have nothing to do with how much you truly are worth in God's eyes. God would give His own Son all over again if He had to reconcile you to Himself. He designed you with a purpose, and keeping yourself pure and free from sexual immorality is one way to honor His purpose and to value yourself as He values you. Never lose sight of how God sees you.

B. How Do You See Yourself? The Power of Self-Respect:

After God, the next person who determines your value is YOU. Whether we acknowledge it or not, our decisions and choices serve as a measuring scale for the value we place on ourselves. We have the capacity to either uphold or diminish the values that God has placed on us when we fail to appropriate them. If only we fully understood the effects of accepting disrespect for our values and boundaries, we would make choices that align only with honor and dignity. Failure to do so can ruin your confidence, self-esteem, and the courage needed to embrace your purpose.

How Do You Represent the Respect You Hold for Yourself?

- **Only entertain relationships that align with your values.** The moment a relationship falls short of your dignity or purity—or even becomes toxic—do not wait for something catastrophic to occur before you realize it is no longer a safe space for you.

- **When you set goals, stick to them.** Some people who come into our lives are sources of distraction and confusion, and you must not compromise your standards or targets to accommodate these diversions.

- **Prioritize and value your time.** If you do not prioritize your time, no one else will. It's that simple. If people realize you have an endless supply of time to waste on meaningless relationships, they will exploit it and drain you until they find the next interesting thing. Learn to say no when necessary and keep everyone in their proper place in your life. Do not make long-term choices with temporary people.

- **Protect your peace and avoid 'situation-ships.'** Often, when faced with the choice between preserving your peace and entertaining drama, you are met with manipulations and accusations that force you to stick with chaos. Protecting your peace means distancing yourself from those who bring confusion, disrespect, and emotional turmoil into your life, and ultimately walking away from any relationship that does not align with who you are.

- **Don't downplay your appearance.** Always present yourself well, as your appearance is the first introduction before anyone even speaks with you. If you present yourself as someone without dignity, you will be treated as such; on the other hand, if you show up as a person with self-respect, you will earn respect. Also, maintain good posture and stand tall—your body language reveals much about how you see yourself.

- **Do not neglect your physical and mental well-being.** Eat healthy meals, exercise regularly, maintain a consistent self-care routine, get adequate rest regardless of how hard you work, go for regular checkups, and seek help when necessary. Your well-being and the effort you invest in it are non-negotiable.

- **Invest in knowledge and skills.** Personal growth is one of the most profound ways to demonstrate your value. Whether you are improving in areas where you lag or exploring new fields, investing in yourself shows how much belief you have in your potential and the person God created you to be.

CHAPTER FIVE

CLARIFYING THE FALSE NARRATIVES THE WORLD TELLS ABOUT SEX

People always say, "If you tell a lie repeatedly, and tell it loud enough, it slowly begins to seem like the truth…" The lies the world tells are convincing, persuasive, loud, and very relentless when it comes to premarital sex. Everywhere you turn, the portrayal of erotic content—whether through advertisements or programs designed to manipulate the thought processes of people in general and the young mind specifically—thwarts their purpose.

"As water wears away the stones and floods wash away the soil, so you destroy people's hope." – Job 14:19

These contents are projected unrelentingly through TV series, music, movies, news, social media, and other platforms. With the advent of social media, billions of dollars are expended yearly to keep the lies going. These are the realities of this generation, and there is no sign of slowing down anytime soon. After some time, the lies being peddled begin to seem like reality; it is no wonder Scripture says faith comes by hearing—and so does unbelief and all immoral products from the kingdom of darkness. Waiting until you are mature and more experienced to have sex is now considered old-fashioned. The heartbreaking part of these lies is that they are not only misleading but also dangerous.

Lie No. 01 – "Sex proves love."

Sex and love are mostly considered synonyms, and that is a fallacy. True love satisfies and endures—it goes far beyond sexual intercourse. The tingling in your body and the cravings to peel off your clothes are not love. Love sprouts from true commitment, respect for one another, loyalty, and selflessness. "Love is patient, love is kind. It does not envy, it does not boast, it is not proud. It does not dishonor others, it is not self-seeking, it is not easily angered, it keeps no record of wrongs. Love does not delight in evil but rejoices with the truth. It always protects, always trusts, always hopes, always perseveres." *1 Corinthians 13:4-7*

People mostly go into relationships because of the body they see and the sex they look forward to, and this makes it difficult to find fulfillment or true commitment in these relationships. A study published in the Journal of Sex Research proves that people who find themselves in relationships revolving around sex (and not love) exhibit low self-esteem and regret, compared to those who practice intimacy in wholesome relationships. While society tells us that careless sex is a sign of love, God intends sex to be a covenant between a man and a wife, and anything that works against that is bound for chaos.

Lie No. 02 – "If you don't explore, you won't find yourself."

When we interact with others—whether on a platonic level or on an erotic level—there is every tendency to gain new insights into things or people through those interactions. This may add to our knowledge or sometimes give us new perspectives on things we already know, but it does not necessarily translate into a complete shift in our identity. Your identity can never be discovered by the number of times you have had sex or by how many partners you have had; it can only be established through finding your individual purpose in life—your unique path, which ultimately has its root in your Creator.

38

Therefore, when Scripture says, "In Him we live, we move and have our being," it should register the reality that without Him, we are nothing. Social experiments—such as exploring the workability of a future with someone solely through cohabitation—do not guarantee success because the guardrails of commitment and law are missing, and those are the very guardrails within which marriages thrive.

Understand this lie as a trap and know that while experimenting may seem exciting, you do not need other people's validation to be what God says you will be. Do not waste your time chasing people and assuming you will find yourself in them; invest that energy into exploring your gifts, talents, passions, and faith in God, and you will discover who you really are. "For we are God's handiwork, created in Christ Jesus to do good works, which God prepared in advance for us to do." – *Ephesians 2:10*

Your identity is rooted in the fact that you were created with intention and purpose—not by trial and error.

Lie No. 03 – "There is no harm in casual sex or relationships."

It's common to hear people say, "Don't worry, we're just having fun and there are no strings attached." That is a pathetic lie they tell themselves to feel better. In truth, there are lots of strings attached. Every relationship we enter into has an effect on us, whether we realize it or not. Imagine gluing two pieces of paper together and then trying to separate them. It doesn't go as smoothly as when you glued them, does it?

Each time you become intimate with someone and then part ways, it leaves both of you wounded, with a part of you remaining with each other. Moreover, over time you become so torn that when you eventually decide to settle down with your spouse, it becomes almost impossible to offer a whole, unbroken version of yourself because you are burdened with emotional holes and baggage from your past. So yes, there are always strings attached.

Proverbs 4:23 tells us, "Above all else, guard your heart, for everything you do flows from it."

Lie No. 04 – "If you love me, you'll give me your body."

This misconception is nothing but manipulation aimed at stealing your most valuable "gold," and it mostly comes from a swine. If you're not firm in your decisions, you find yourself trapped into selling your soul for validation simply because you believe you are in love.

When the handshake goes beyond the elbow, run was what we were told then—and I say the same to you today. True love understands boundaries and is not selfish.

Lie No. 05 – "You're wasting your time. Everyone does it sooner or later."

The world makes you believe that everyone is having premarital sex just to make you feel out of place. They paint premarital sex as unavoidable and inevitable.

However, while the number of people upholding this narrative is alarming, there is also a great number of self-aware individuals who are intentionally choosing to remain unstained and wait until marriage to enjoy sex the way God approves of it. It's okay not to follow the noise.

In *1 Peter 1:16*, God tells us, "Be holy, because I am holy." Waiting is very possible and always worth it.

Lie No. 06 – "Waiting is a burden."

When it comes to sex, people around us often downplay the importance of self-control. They chase instant gratification and, worst of all, make self-control seem like a sad burden. It makes one wonder: when did having self-control ever become a burden? Purity comes with long-lasting rewards that will always outweigh the temporary pleasure from casual sex.

A study conducted by the University of Chicago found that couples who waited until marriage to have sex reported significantly higher levels of happiness and sexual fulfillment in their relationships. Why? Because their foundation was built on trust, communication, and emotional intimacy—not fleeting physical attraction.

The world portrays waiting as a burden, but it is an investment. By waiting, you protect your heart, preserve your self-worth, and set yourself up for a future relationship built on respect and mutual honor. As Jesus said in *John 10:10*: "The thief comes only to steal and kill and destroy; I have come that they may have life and have it to the full."

Lie No. 07 – "It's your body and you can do whatever you wish."

Humans have free will to make their own choices, but they often fail to remember that we do not own our bodies because we did not create ourselves. Our bodies belong to the Maker, not to us, and are not ours to explore as we please.

Prioritizing spiritual obedience must always come before personal desires for God's chosen people. Do you not know that your body is the temple of the Holy Ghost, which is in you and which you have from God, and that you are not your own? For you were bought with a price; therefore glorify God in your body and in your spirit, which are God's. When you finally realize that your body is God's sacred temple, you begin to see why your choices must reflect God's holiness, purity, and love for you.

Lie No. 08 – "If you ever made a mistake before now, there's no point in stopping now."

Many feel guilty and unworthy of God's forgiveness and love because of this stinking lie. But who did Christ come for? The righteous, or to reconcile sinners to God? Saying there is no going back once you've made a mistake is a trap meant to keep you in sin. And the more time you waste in sin, the more ruin

41

you bring upon yourself. Paul asks, "Shall we continue to sin so that grace may abound?" Of course not, because if that happens, we take the grace of God for granted.

God's mercy knows no bounds, and no matter the mistake you think you've made, He will put you back together again. Do not let yourself rot away in self-condemnation. *Psalm 103:12* reassures us of God's forgiveness when it says:

"As far as the east is from the west, so far has He removed our transgressions from us.".

Never forget that your mistake can be corrected only if you find your way back to the Father and genuinely allow Him to transform your life. No matter the damage done, it is not too late to start afresh and save your future.

Jeremiah 29:11 tells us of God's plan:

"For I know the plans I have for you," declares the Lord, "plans to prosper you and not to harm you, plans to give you hope and a future."

Trusting God with your future means honoring Him with your present choices.

Lie No. 09 – "Sex completes you as an adult."

This lie seeks to deceive people into believing that sexual intimacy is the solution to emotional voids. A girl with an absentee father might try to fill that vacuum with immoral relationships. Likewise, some men may assume sex is what completes them or gives their lives meaning. Yet, what happens is that they have tons of sex with people of different shapes, sizes, and races, and still, the emptiness only grows worse. They end up lonely in the midst of plenty and sad with fake smiles on their lips. *Psalm 16:11* reminds us:

"You make known to me the path of life; you will fill me with joy in your presence, with eternal pleasures in your right hand."

Fulfillment comes from walking in God's purpose and experiencing His joy, not from temporary pleasures. Searching for completion through sexual relationships leads to the worst kinds of disappointment. *Colossians 2:10* tells us, "And you have been made complete in Christ," who is the head over every ruler and authority.

Lie No. 10 – "You're not Jesus Christ. You need to enjoy yourself because God knows you can't overcome temptations."

This particular lie strips listeners of their faith in God's grace and sustenance. However, God has reassured us that He will never leave us alone in our struggles and that His grace is sufficient to carry us through. "No temptation has overtaken you except what is common to mankind. And God is faithful; He will not let you be tempted beyond what you can bear. But when you are tempted, He will also provide a way out so that you can endure it." *1 Corinthians 10:13*

God always provides a way to resist temptation. With prayer, accountability, and reliance on His strength, victory is possible.

These aren't all the lies society tries to shove into our heads, but the Spirit of God will always be there to help you discern the lies that emerge from the pit of hell to trap our lives and thwart our destinies. By identifying and countering these lies, you can walk in truth, protect your heart, and align your life with God's purpose. Waiting isn't deprivation—it's an earnest preparation for the mindful life God has planned for you.

Practical Wisdom to Counter These Lies

"And ye shall know the truth, and the truth shall make you free." *John 8:32*

The devil loves to manipulate and deceive with lies and half-truths, but God has given you the Holy Spirit for discernment, wisdom, and faith. Understanding the lies is only one part; you must also be grounded in ways to stay safe from their traps. Consider the following steps as your guide:

1. **Choose a Like-Minded Support System**

   Be around friends, mentors, and believers in a community that promotes purity and godly living. An accountability partner can help you stay committed and motivated to achieve your life goals.

2. **Be Thrilled to Embark on the Journey**

   Living a life in accordance with God's Word gives you freedom, peace, and the gift of the Holy Spirit. Celebrate your spiritual growth as every step brings you closer to God's perfect plan for your life.

3. **Keep Growing Your Understanding of God's Word**

   Enrich your mind with God's words. *Romans 12:2* says, "Do not conform to the pattern of this world, but be transformed by the renewing of your mind." The more you immerse yourself in Scripture, the more power you have to overcome the world's deceits and temptations.

4. **Be Highly Selective of What Influences You**

   Be mindful of the media you consume, the friends you surround yourself with, and the environments you frequent. Surround yourself with positive people and content that uplifts your commitment to the ways of your Maker.

5. **Keep Your Eyes on the Reward of Tomorrow**

   Do not only think about today; consider your future. What you do today dictates what your future will be. Before taking an important step, ask yourself: Will this choice bring me closer to my life goals? Does it honor God and His purpose for me? For instance, a young woman named Mary in the Bible chose to remain pure despite peer pressure. She was not only pure in body but also pure of heart. God saw the great life she lived and chose her to give birth to our Lord Jesus Christ.

6. **Have Absolute Trust in the Plans of God**

God has the best plans for you—better than any plans you have for yourself. He loves you dearly, more than anyone ever could. Trust Him, abide by His will, and live a life that aligns with His purpose. Trust that His ways are higher than yours (*Isaiah 55:8-9*).

7. **Take Your Eyes Off the World and Its Patterns**

Your choices today significantly impact your future. While the world focuses on short-term pleasure, God wants you to store your treasures in heaven. *Matthew 6:19-21* instructs, "Do not lay up for yourselves treasures on earth, where moth and rust destroy and where thieves break in and steal, but lay up for yourselves treasures in heaven, where neither moth nor rust destroys and where thieves do not break in and steal. For where your treasure is, there your heart will be also." Waiting for God's timing is an act of obedience that yields everlasting blessings.

As the world continues to be louder about sex, you should not engage in its deception. You have chosen to honor God with your body and your life, and that is profoundly rewarding. You are protecting yourself from the immorality of life and setting your life on a path for a meaningful relationship that honors God.

Let the words of Jesus always resound in your heart. When you walk in truth, you experience the freedom, joy, and peace that the world can never offer. Choose the truth. Choose purity. Choose God's best for your life.

By overcoming these lies with God's Word—which is truth—you enable yourself to live a fulfilling life. Jesus came so we could have power over sin and overcome the world and its deceit. Avoid the fake promises of your peers. Choose God, and experience the fullness of the great life God has for you.

CHAPTER SIX

LOVE AND LUST: THE BATTLE OF THE MIND

In the spring, at the time when kings go off to war, David sent Joab out with the king's men and the whole Israelite army. They destroyed the Ammonites and besieged Rabbah. But David remained in Jerusalem. One evening David got up from his bed and walked around on the roof of the palace. From the roof he saw a woman bathing. The woman was very beautiful, and David sent someone to find out about her. The man said, "She is Bathsheba, the daughter of Eliam and the wife of Uriah the Hittite."

Then David sent messengers to get her. She came to him, and he slept with her. (Now she was purifying herself from her monthly uncleanness.) Then she went back home. (2 Samuel 11:1–4).

Every major battle in life will be won or lost first in the mind. The mind is the birthplace of thoughts—or call them ideas—and, in essence, the pivot for the trajectory of a man's life. You must think of something before it can be an action, no matter how many microseconds were at your disposal before you took that action. David probably did not get out of his bed to look for Bathsheba on that particular day. He might have been trying to meditate about whatever was going on in his life or simply seeking time to be alone. What changed? One of the gates to the mind was open—and that was his eyes; that was not the problem, but rather the state of his mind was the issue.

Proverbs 4:23, 25

"Guard your heart more than anything else, because the source of your life flows from it. Let your eyes look straight ahead, and keep your sight focused in front of you."

David missed two things in this scenario.

- He was not looking straight ahead, as he was admonished—not literally (i.e., "looking straight" means keeping his focus on his purpose and God's plan for him)—but his eyes went somewhere else. He was not looking unto the Author and Finisher of his salvation.

- The disastrous part was that something else was in control of his mind at the time. That means that something else was in control of his thoughts, emotions, and, in effect, his life.

James 1:14–15

"Temptation comes from our own desires, which entice us and drag us away. These desires give birth to sinful actions. And when sin is allowed to grow, it gives birth to death."

There was nothing wrong with him seeing Bathsheba from the top of the palace if he had immediately controlled the thought process in his mind from that point—especially through the well of the word of God that was in him—but at that time, he had lost control. His mind was in the wrong places, and he was following all the suggestions his mind was giving him, so he went ahead and made all those thoughts a reality.

All these didn't just happen overnight. His thought process had been lost before he saw Bathsheba. Sometimes people cook up ideas—especially if a Christian falls into fornication or adultery—and when it gets to the point of discussing it, they point accusing fingers like, "She seduced me." To that, my response would always be: if you throw a hook into a river and the fish is covered with a glass-like porcelain insulator, there will be nowhere for the hook to catch the fish. That is the scenario. David must have thought about having more women in addition to the ones he already had, so he could explore whatever fun he was hoping to get from such activities. The simple thing the devil did was to help him get the kind of woman that would catch his attention—one who would be nearby where David would always be.

David's case shows us what lust looks like. He was informed that she was the wife of one of his commanders right off the bat. That should have made him draw back, but at that moment he was not the one doing the thinking. His penis was doing the thinking for him. If a man was putting his life on the line for you on the battlefield, the least you could do as their leader was to make sure that all they had worked hard for—and their families—were safe. Absolute betrayal, and no other reason than that he was not in charge at that moment.

A. The Destructive Nature of Lust – Lessons From The Story of David.

1. Lust often leads to wickedness, deception, and more layers of sin, as in David's lust which led to manipulation and murder.

2. Lust should be taken seriously because it brings a lot of harm and room for evil if not carefully checked and corrected. As upright as David was prior to this time, his lust caused him to commit adultery and break God's commandment without second thoughts.

3. Allowing your eyes to linger where they shouldn't be would, most times, cause your unhealthy desires to take control. By entertaining lustful thoughts, we can be led into a web of complications that would be difficult to undo.

4. We set ourselves up for temptation by not being diligent and purposeful in our places of duty. Idleness is usually an opening for sin.

David was supposed to be in the field with his army behind him, but instead, he stayed back and found his way into temptation.

5. Lust often leads to abuse of power, where people manipulate their positions to have their way—just as in the case of David. The repercussion of this filthy action is that God sees even the innermost content of a man's heart and his intentions. Even though forgiveness may come later, the consequences will always be excruciating.

B. What Is Love?

Love can be described as a genuine affection and care for another person that is deep, unselfish, and sacrificial. While love is mostly deemed as just an emotion of wanting or caring for someone, it is rather more of an intentional decision to cherish, honor, and keep someone safe.

The Greek language, for example, has different words for different kinds of love, and they are: Agape, which is sacrificial love (like the type of love Jesus had when He gave Himself for us and expects us to do the same for others); Storge, which is the kind of love that exists between parents and children and among family members in general; Philia, the love that exists between brothers or among friends—a kind of love developed out of mutual respect; and finally, Eros, the romantic kind of love which involves physical attraction.

1 Corinthians 13:4–7

"Love is patient, love is kind. It does not envy, it does not boast, it is not proud. It does not dishonor others, it is not self-seeking, it is not easily angered, it keeps no record of wrongs. Love does not delight in evil but rejoices with the truth. It always protects, always trusts, always hopes, always perseveres."

Paul's definition of love from the above scriptures shows agape love. John 3:16 tells us of the greatest love story ever known—of how much God loves the world; hence, He had to send His only begotten Son to die for our sins just to reconcile us to Himself.

In Genesis 29:20 as well, Jacob and Rachel portray love from the perspective of endurance. Seven years was nothing when Jacob had to work to marry Rachel because of his genuine love for her. Lust wouldn't have endured that but would have moved on to someone else, thinking it wasn't worth it; yet, Jacob's love was not just patient but sacrificial.

Lust, on the other hand, drives at the urge to satisfy one's selfish, self-centered, and impatient desires. Ammon and Tamar in 2 Samuel 13 is a good example of lust's destructive nature. Ammon was infatuated by the beauty of his half-sister Tamar, but his feelings were brazen lust, not love. He was not in love with her but manipulated her and forcefully raped her when she brought him food while he pretended to be sick. Afterwards, Ammon hated Tamar more than he had loved her before the rape.

C. Love and Lust Are Polar Opposites, But They Have Certain Similarities That Can Leave One Confused or Mix Up the Two

- They both involve strong affections toward each other. Both love and lust can evoke strong feelings of passion, desire, and attachment, and these emotions can make it hard to distinguish between the two, especially early in a relationship.

- Both love and lust have a common desire to be around each other. Love and lust both spark a longing to be with the other person. However, while love desires emotional, spiritual, and physical closeness, lust focuses almost exclusively on the physical.

- Both love and lust create an overwhelming feeling of longing, but the outcome decides which is which. The initial stages of both love and lust can be overwhelming, filling you with excitement and nervous energy. However, while love deepens over time, lust often fades as quickly as it began.

D. Key Differences Between Love and Lost that Should Never be Taken for Granted

1. While lust is impulsive and hasty, love takes its time. (1 Cor. 13:4)

2. Lust usually looks for what it can get, while love seeks how it can give. (John 3:16)

3. Love builds trust, genuine respect, and intimacy in its purest form, while lust ruins or destroys these elements because of selfish interests.

4. Lust does not have any regard for the other party; love upholds honor and dignity. "Be devoted to one another in love. Honor one another above yourselves." (Romans 12:10)

5. Love creates peace and emotional satisfaction, while lust brings anxiety, chaos, and trauma. (Romans 8:6)

E. How to Always Know if it's Lust You're Dealing With, or Love

1. Speak to yourself and answer certain questions honestly: Is this person helping me to grow closer to God?

2. Evaluate the things they do: How much do they respect my beliefs, personality, or boundaries?

3. Examine your intentions: Are you seeking to instantly quench a longing, or do you wish to build a future together?

F. Practical Ways to Walk In Love

I. Guard Your Heart

Proverbs 4:23 tells us, "Above all else, guard your heart, for everything you do flows from it." Be careful about the things you listen to, the content you read, the conversations you engage in, and the person you are in a relationship with.

II. Set Clear Boundaries

Have clear boundaries to protect yourself from certain things that may have a negative impact on your life. Let your standards align with the words of God.

III. Seek God's Guidance

Always seek God's guidance on any relationship journey you want to embark on. Ask God any questions you may have; He loves you, and He will always be there to assist you in any way you want Him to.

IV. Surround Yourself with Accountability

Build relationships with people who can help you in your pursuit of purity. Feel free to seek advice from your mentors or parents who have experience and can guide you on the right path.

G. Steps to Consider When Looking out for the Purest Form of Love

✓ Compare and study how love is meant to be in 1 Corinthians 13 and follow other examples from the scriptures. Let God's Word guide your understanding of love in your relationships.

✓ Ask for God's gift of discernment so that you can recognize the difference between love and lust. Pray for the strength to walk away from any relationship that's based on lust and pursue the one that's built on love.

✓ Build a strong friendship first before diving into a romantic relationship. Friendship will help you understand each other deeply. True love usually grows out of good friendship.

Summary

Even though these two things have certain similarities, their repercussions are like fire and rain—different. However, understanding what love and lust look like will help you stay on the right path and choose what's best for your destiny. John 10:10: "The thief comes only to steal and kill and destroy; I have come that they may have life and have it to the full." Lust is a thief—it steals purity, kills trust, and destroys hearts. Love, however, brings life in abundance. Choosing love will always keep you honoring God and truly valuing the person you love.

CHAPTER SEVEN

A HOLISTIC APPROACH TO PURITY THAT IS BEYOND SEXUALITY – NURTURING GODLY FRIENDSHIPS AND RELATIONSHIPS

We've all heard the saying, "Show me your friends, and I'll show you who you truly are." This statement highlights a profound truth: the people we surround ourselves with greatly influence our character, values, and direction in life. When we hear the word "purity," it's often associated with sexuality.

However, purity is much broader than abstaining from sexual immorality. True biblical purity encompasses every aspect of our lives: our thoughts, words, actions, and our daily associations. It's a daily, intentional pursuit of reflecting God's holiness in all we do. Friendships and relationships have the power to either encourage you in your walk with God or lead you down paths of compromise.

Achieving holistic purity entails bringing your body, mind, and emotions into harmony with God's will. Avoiding sexual immorality is only one aspect of it. Every decision you take daily should actively pursue righteousness, honesty, compassion, and love. When we follow this path, our way of life will ultimately demonstrate our devotion to Christ. "Blessed are the pure in heart, for they shall see God." (Matthew 5:8)

1. **Purity In Thoughts – Protecting Our Minds**

Temptations, anxieties, and immoral thoughts frequently target our minds, which are like a battlefield. Purity in thinking involves our conscious concentration on what is honorable, true, and pure.

How to Protect Your Mind

a. Reflect on the undiluted Word of God for His leading. Reading the Bible and listening to inspiring messages feeds our minds and shields our imaginations from negative thoughts, desires, and influences. "Be transformed by the renewing of your mind, and do not conform to the pattern of this world." (Romans 12:2)

b. Steer clear of toxic or unhealthy media. Our thoughts are influenced by the things we invest our eyes and ears on. Pay attention to what you read, watch, and hear. For instance, if a certain channel you are watching on TV suddenly starts displaying unhealthy content, it may be time to switch to a more positive TV program. c. Always be thankful to God for how far He has sustained you. Consciously develop an attitude of gratitude. Substitute thankfulness for pessimistic or envious thoughts.

In simple terms, it is important to note that your personality and actions are like a garden, while your mind is the fertile soil. This implies that whatever seeds you plant will bloom in abundance. It doesn't matter if they're good or bad. Hence, negative thoughts equal a negative life/reality, and godly or pure thoughts equal a beautiful harvest of righteousness.

2. **Purity In Our Speech – Speaking Grace-Filled Words**

Think of when God created the universe. He spoke, and it became everything He uttered. Most times we don't realize how powerful our words are as children of God. Our simple utterances can raise someone up or ruin them; hence, it is our place to consistently speak life, hope, love, healing, kindness, godliness, and purity to everyone around us. "Let no unwholesome talk come out of your mouths, but only what is helpful for building others up according to their needs." (Ephesians 4:29)

3. **Being Pure In Our Deeds – Living A Life of Integrity**

Our actions and deeds portray purity when these actions align with the ways of God. How do you treat others? How do you react to challenges? And most importantly, do your actions align with God's commandments? Purity in actions means aligning your behavior with God's commandments. This includes how you treat others, how you use your time, and how you respond to challenges. "The integrity of the upright guides them, but the unfaithful are destroyed by their duplicity." (Proverbs 11:3)

In a world that often prioritizes superficial connections, building godly friendships and relationships can be a challenge. Yet, these relationships are critical to living a life that honors God and fulfilling your God-given purpose.

4. **Being Pure In Relationships – The Point In Surrounding Ourselves With Like-minded People**

A. Our Friends Positively or Negatively Influence Our Behaviors

"Do not be misled: 'Bad company corrupts good character.'" (1 Corinthians 15:33)

Also, 1 Kings 11:4 shows us how King Solomon, who was known for his wisdom, eventually compromised his commitment and devotion to the Almighty God after he started relating with pagan wives. They led him to their idols.

B. They hold us Accountable and Encourage Us to stay on the Right Path

"As iron sharpens iron, so one person sharpens another." (Proverbs 27:17)

Sometimes we are prone to certain mistakes and weaknesses, but the Holy Spirit nudges us and sends help through our godly associates to remain upright.

C. They Render Encouragement in Difficult Times

"Therefore encourage one another and build each other up…" (1 Thessalonians 5:11)

Jonathan and David's friendship in the book of 1 Samuel 18:1-4 portrays how relevant and impactful our friends can be when chasing a course.

How to look out for Red Flags in Our Associations and Avoid Temptations

Now that we understand the importance of choosing healthy relationships, below are critical red flags to be wary of.

1. **They Encourage Compromise**

   If someone pressures you to lower your standards, engage in sinful behavior, or ignore God's principles, this is a clear sign that the relationship is unhealthy.

Bible Verse: "Blessed is the one who does not walk in step with the wicked or stand in the way that sinners take or sit in the company of mockers." (Psalm 1:1)

Example: In Judges 16, Samson's relationship with Delilah serves as a cautionary tale. Her constant manipulation led Samson to compromise his calling, resulting in devastating consequences.

2. **They Lack Respect for Your Values**

A godly relationship should honor your convictions. If someone dismisses or mocks your faith and values, they are not helping you grow closer to God.

3. **They Bring Chaos Instead of Peace**

Any relationship that doesn't come with clarity but brings constant heartache, confusion, and drama is unhealthy for your mental and spiritual health. A healthy relationship brings peace, joy, and clarity— not constant drama, confusion, or turmoil. God is a God of peace, and relationships that are chaotic often indicate they are not aligned with His will.

"For God is not a God of disorder but of peace." (1 Corinthians 14:33)

4. **They Make You Forsake God**

It's quite common to meet people who don't do the will of God and have no regard for His commandments. They not only love worldly things but also encourage people around them to follow their path. They may ridicule your godly lifestyle, question your faith in God, and encourage you to engage in activities that are contrary to the words of God.

There is an adage that says, "When the sheep develop a fondness for walking with a dog, the sheep will form the habit of consuming feces."

For instance, your wild friend might convince you to skip going to church on Sunday for a party or a hangout with a party of friends. They have no regard for your spiritual relationship with God, and they're not ready to emulate your spiritual life. In fact, it gives them extreme joy and satisfaction when they make you derail from purity.

"Blessed is the man that walketh not in the counsel of the ungodly, nor standeth in the way of sinners, nor sitteth in the seat of the scornful. But his delight is in the law of the Lord; and in his law doth he meditate day and night." (Psalm 1:1-3)

5. **They Are Controlling or Manipulative**

Anyone who tries to make you act against God's doctrine, control your decisions, and manipulate you emotionally doesn't love you and has zero respect for you. This is not godly love. Godly love is unconditional, enduring, kind, forgiving, and caring. Love never fails, but people fail love. When relationships and marriages fail, they tend to blame love: "He never loved me; he stopped loving me." They blame everything on love but forget that love never fails—it's people that fail love.

There are many so-called expressions of love in the world today, but pure godly love is what you should seek. It's pure godly love when someone loves you and your God, when they make you move closer to God and not away from Him. Anyone who makes you embark on a journey that is wild, worldly, and ungodly will eventually make you forsake God. Someone who tries to control your decisions, isolate you from others, or manipulate you emotionally is not acting out of love or respect. This behavior often reflects insecurity or selfishness, not godly love.

Example: Delilah manipulated Samson (Judges 16:15-16), wearing him down emotionally to achieve her own selfish goals.

6. **They Facilitate Hatred and Negativity**

Relationships built on gossip, backbiting, or reveling in the downfall of others are doomed to fail. Every relationship must be built on love, and because God is love, such a relationship lasts forever. The pillar of every relationship is important; hence, we must genuinely answer this question: What brings you together? Is it backbiting or gossip? This is essential because it will dictate whether things go well or end up being one terrible decision you've ever made.

"Do not let any unwholesome talk come out of your mouths, but only what is helpful for building others up." (Ephesians 4:29)

7. **They Don't Give You Room For Your Personal Endeavors**

A healthy relationship cares for, values, and respects your physical, emotional, and spiritual boundaries. Your relationship shouldn't make you lose your true self; rather, it should help you discover yourself. If someone puts you under the pressure of always doing things that please them, with no regard for your feelings or respect for your boundaries, it's a serious red flag. You need to be meticulous in choosing the people you want to be with.

For instance: A friend who constantly does things they know you hate and ignores your feelings shows a lack of love for you. "Flee from sexual immorality. All other sins a person commits are outside the body, but whoever sins sexually, sins against their own body." (1 Corinthians 6:18)

8. **They Are Self-Centered**

Most people believe that relationships are meant to satisfy their own personal needs. They talk about themselves all the time, and when they have problems, they seek help from you. They do not care about what you're going through—only about themselves. True friendship or love is sacrificial and mutual, not self-centered.

"Do nothing out of selfish ambition or vain conceit. Rather, in humility, value others above yourselves." (Philippians 2:3)

9. They Promote Unhealthy Habits

Unhealthy habits are everywhere in the world today, and it's the trend of the day. Unhealthy habits are often adopted from bad friends because bad company corrupts good character. If someone encourages harmful habits such as hard drugs, excessive partying, or immoral dressing, they are not helping you honor your body as God's temple.

Your body is the temple of God—a body that doesn't honor God is doomed for destruction. For instance, hard drugs can cause psychotic behavior, seizures, or death due to overdose. Living a godly life is for your own benefit; it's not really for God's benefit. God loves you— hence why He gave you His Holy Spirit to distinguish between what is good and bad, so we can live healthy lives.

"Do you not know that your bodies are temples of the Holy Spirit, who is in you, whom you have received from God? You are not your own." (1 Corinthians 6:19)

10. They Create Division and Strife

People who constantly cause division among friends, stir up arguments, or create drama can hinder your peace and growth in Christ. Jesus Christ taught us to be peaceful and not violent. "Blessed are the peacemakers, for they will be called children of God." (Matthew 5:9)

11. **They Lack a Desire for Spiritual Growth**

It's very important to be with someone who helps you grow spiritually. It's not wise to be with someone hostile toward God's word and your spiritual growth. They may get angry when you read the Bible or attend Bible studies. They want you to be like them and join in doing worldly things. Such people are not good for you, and it can be challenging to maintain a relationship grounded in godly love.

Example: King Ahab and Queen Jezebel—Jezebel's pagan influence led Ahab further away from God (1 Kings 21:25-26).

12. **They Do Not Celebrate Your Wins**

True friends and partners are happy about your success and are willing to assist you in achieving your goals. If someone is resentful of your achievements, it shows that they do not love you. People who are resentful about your achievements are not people you should be around, because they'd do anything to see your downfall. "Rejoice with those who rejoice; mourn with those who mourn." (Romans 12:15)

13. **They Pressure You into Quick Decisions**

Healthy relationships allow patience and provide room for thoughtful decisions. If someone pressures you into doing things against your will, it's a red flag. Remember your self-worth and do not settle for less. Healthy relationships allow for patience and thoughtful decisions. If someone pressures you into making rash commitments or life-altering choices, it's a red flag.

Example: In Genesis 25:29-34, Esau made a rash decision to sell his birthright for a meal, leading to lasting regret.

14. **They Lack Humility and Forgiveness**

There are times when we hurt people we love and they hurt us too—these things happen. Relationships require the willingness to forgive and forget.

"Be kind and compassionate to one another, forgiving each other, just as in Christ God forgave you." (Ephesians 4:32)

15. **They Discourage Your Purpose**

Our purpose does not always make sense to some people around us, but people shouldn't feel comfortable trivializing or making jokes about God's purpose in your life. God places a calling and purpose on each of our lives. If someone belittles your dreams or discourages you from pursuing God's plan, they are not aligned with His will for you.

What You Can Do When You Notice These Red Flags

1. **Pray for Guidance**

Pray to God for the spirit of discernment and wisdom to recognize whether a relationship is helping or hindering your spiritual growth. "If any of you lacks wisdom, you should ask God, who gives generously to all without finding fault, and it will be given to you." (James 1:5)

2. **Seek Godly Counsel**

Feel free to seek advice from your trusted mentor, pastor, or godly friend.

Proverbs 11:14 reminds us: "For lack of guidance a nation falls, but victory is won through many advisers."

Building godly friendships and relationships takes intentionality, prayer, and discernment. By recognizing these red flags and seeking God's guidance, you can cultivate connections that honor Him and support your journey toward His purpose for your life.

Examples of Positive Friendships and Relationships

1. **Ruth and Naomi**

   Ruth and Naomi had a relationship based on loyalty, trust, and mutual support. Despite obstacles, they cared for and encouraged each other.

2. **Paul and Timothy**

   Paul groomed Timothy in God, helping him grow in his faith in the Lord. They shared strong faith and commitment, which helped advance the kingdom of God. (2 Timothy 1:2-6)

3. **A Trusted Christian Community**

   The early church in Acts 2:42-47 showed us what Christian relationships should be like. They shared what they had in love and unity, and prayed together in one accord. This helped them grow deeply in Christ, and when the time came, they were all endowed with the Holy Spirit.

Practical Ways to Build Relationships That Are Godly

1. **Pray for The Spirit Of Discernment**

   Ask God to lead you to people who will help you grow spiritually and in faith. Your prayer will align your heart with God's will for your life and invite the Holy Spirit to take control of your relationships. "Ask and it will be given to you; seek and you will find; knock and the door will be opened to you." (Matthew 7:7)

2. **Be The Friend You Would Love To Have**

Be what you want your friends to be. Before seeking godly friends, strive to become one. Practice love, kindness, patience, and humility in your interactions with others.

"So in everything, do to others what you would have them do to you." (Matthew 7:12)

3. **Join Believers' Communities**

   Surround yourself with like-minded believers by attending church, Bible studies, or Christian events. These environments provide opportunities to form meaningful connections that promote a godly life.

4. **Create Healthy Boundaries**

   Safeguard your heart by establishing boundaries that honor God. Communicate your values clearly and refuse to compromise them.

5. **Evaluate Your Relationships Constantly**

   Take time to assess your friendships and relationships. Ask yourself: Are they helping you grow spiritually, drawing you closer to God, or pulling you away from Him? Be willing to let go of relationships that hinder your spiritual growth.

The Reward In Meticulously Handpicked Friendships or Bonds

When you associate yourself with godly people, you grow spiritually and in love. These relationships can improve your life; as you grow spiritually, you are blessed with the spirit of discernment and truth. Building godly relationships is more rewarding than worldly relationships.

They can be your support system through anything you experience. Being with people who honor God helps you understand what true love is and the blessings that come with it.

Living an upright life that is blameless before God—and embodying holiness—will always give you a better version of yourself. You'll be amazed at how happy and fulfilled you become.

CHAPTER EIGHT

HOW TO COME AROUND DATING IN A HOOK-UP-INFESTED GENERATION

Dating before the age of mobile phones or social media was usually restricted to the local community, where people were introduced to one another through friends, family, and acquaintances. But in this technological age, people are thousands of miles apart and are dating. This comes with quite a number of challenges—especially differences in culture—and the most important reason for dating, getting to know the person, can be challenging, particularly if they are not truthful about who they are. This is why it is essential to be more intentional, to tread carefully while trying to get to know people, and, most of all, to be prayerful. If the person you are trying to get to know does not want to be known, then all you are likely to get out of the dating process could be chaff and no substance, and you do not want to invest your time and emotion into a venture that will not be fruitful in the end. Dating can be a powerful tool to help you navigate the future you envision when it is correctly handled.

Dating in a society that glamorizes casual sex, hookups, sex hawking, and normalized prostitution can be challenging and confusing—especially if you want to be intentional as a child of God and follow the patterns laid out in

Scripture.

Myles Munroe once analyzed the process of dating as a time to get to know your would-be partner spiritually and emotionally before getting to the physical, which should come much later. However, that has been turned the other way, in the sense that the first thing this generation explores about their partner is the physical. That is how the question of casual sex exists in the first place. Look at it from this perspective: if you meet a guy or a girl and you want to start dating, there is supposed to be a time to try to get to know who they are as a person—what they believe and how much their faith affects the decisions they make—before exploring any other aspect of their lives. If you both have opposite opinions about faith, that might already be a problem for a future together; but if you do not allow room to find out that part, it will still show up down the line in the relationship, and, if there had not been any previous discussion about how to navigate around it, a crisis could begin—possibly even down the line into marriage.

You also do not want a man or woman who is not emotionally stable and not willing to put in the work to be teachable and grow up emotionally. Having self-control, as the Bible puts it, is not a baby's job. This is true in the sense that people from different backgrounds may show their differences down the line because you were not raised by the same parents—even people who are similar have differences. When your partner is angry and cannot handle a situation, and immediately assumes that your intention is to hurt them, then that might be a problem.

The time it takes to explore both the spiritual and emotional intelligence of the person you are dating—with clarity—must always be before things become physical. Even though emotions may run back and forth because you both are in love, the ability to put affections on hold and pursue the buildup of a friendship with clarity will, in the long run, provide a solid foundation for the relationship. In this process, you can ascertain whether the person's intentions are genuine. Most importantly, over time, you can move the person from just being an acquaintance to being a friend—until you can say with complete assurance that they are your best friend. If someone does not reach that stage, there is no point in moving the relationship into the physical. This might sound like a lot, but exploring this route will save you a headache tomorrow. This was usually the process of dating that most successful marriages today went through to become a success.

Dating today might be very different from the process set forth above, as meeting at a club or party has become the norm for most people. If you meet someone for the first time and they are not in control of their actions—because they have been intoxicated by alcohol and do not know what they are doing—would you want to meet someone you believe would be a very important part of your life in such a situation, or would you prefer to be approached when you are at your strongest? There might be some who met in this manner and it still turned out okay, but wouldn't you want clear eyes when making important decisions about your life? Or would you prefer someone else to simply assume they know what you are thinking when clearly you aren't thinking at all? This is how most people start from the physical, and if your body is the temple of the Holy Ghost, this is not how you would like it to be treated.

In this generation of swiping right and left, liking and commenting online through social media, dating has moved to a new level. The things to focus on while trying to get to know people have slightly changed, coupled with the fact that Hollywood—which serves as an educational medium for many young people—is not equipping these young minds with the tools to effectively choose the right person to date. Shallow characteristics, such as how the person looks, are valued over inner beauty; the number of followers they have is prized over their sense of judgment; and smooth talking is favored over a well-rounded mindset. When the foundation of a building is faulty before it is constructed, it is a disaster waiting to happen. You need, as a matter of urgency, to enter the dating pool with the consciousness to make the right decisions that can effectively support the building of the great future you envision. When the appropriate cautions are not taken—when loving yourself is not prioritized— the aftermath is usually not far from disaster. Take your dating life seriously, because you will be grateful for it in the future.

HOLLYWOOD DATING SUPERMARKET

Dating sites and other promoters of casual sex/hookups preach a certain kind of falsehood that leaves their customers feeling like they're having the time of their lives. They portray it as a liberating, light-hearted, and carefree experience that is devoid of trauma or stress, but fails to reveal the unmet expectations and the void left in the hearts of their victims. It's like a setup where one expects an easy, rosy route to love, intimate bonding, connection, and fulfillment, but ends up in an unexpected hall of disappointments. People end up wound up, bitter, and full of resentment because they followed a playbook they found on television or social media. Some people are just out there trying to gather likes and comments, not necessarily trying to educate you. It would not be their fault if you did not do your due diligence to understand exactly what you are getting into before jumping on something they portrayed as working.

In the hallway of this Hollywood supermarket, "are we exclusive" is another phrase you hear often after heartbreak. This was not even something to think about in those days, but somehow, it has found its way into mainstream media. Please understand that the reason you see someone dating a new person every other month is not because they are serious about getting to know them better—which was supposed to be the purpose of dating—but because they are playing a different game, and that game is an old one. It is called hunting; some people are only trying to taste all kinds of meat they find in the forest. They have no interest in getting to know people because, to them, that is too burdensome. This is not peculiar to any one sex, because both males and females are into the hunting game.

Matthew 7:6

"Give not that which is holy unto the dogs, neither cast ye your pearls before swine, lest they trample them under their feet, and turn again and rend you."

There is a saying that "dress the way you want to be addressed." Do you want to be just a statistic in another person's game, or do you really want to take control of your life and remove it from the control of another person? Because if you let them, they would trample your pearl.

Humans were made to have intimacy and proper relationships. Choosing to 'casualize' sex will always leave you starving for what God intended marriages to be. Some believe that engaging in casual sex over time will help build intimacy and connection, but that's not how meaningful relationships work. It's like waiting for winter to come before deciding to gather your supplies. It's like holding a basket in the rain and hoping for it to fill up—you'll always be stranded.

If the understanding and friendship that are supposed to be the bedrock of any functional relationship haven't been established first, you have no business getting naked in front of the person you think you have a thing for. You'll either end up feeling used or stupid, or you may find yourself in a breakup that requires time to heal.

Why do people go into casual relationships and hookups?

1. **To avoid commitment:** A lot of people want the benefits of being married without being committed to someone, and sex is one of those benefits they seek. These individuals can also use others financially or simply to carry out activities that align with their selfish interests.

2. **As a distraction:** Some people use others to distract themselves, especially after a terrible breakup. They use hookups as a crutch to pass

time and heal from the sadness they feel, moving on and leaving the other party broken as soon as they feel better about themselves.

3. **To experiment:** Sometimes they just want to experiment and see how fun it can be to spend time with many partners within the same period—they are only exploring a game.

4. **For excitement:** Some people find casual sex and hookups exciting, taking advantage of the lack of rules and guidelines. Without the demand for commitment, it's like a freeway ride to have as much fun as possible.

5. **To avoid emotional risk:** Others choose casual relationships because they're scared of risking their emotions and getting hurt.

How Should We Handle Dating and Relationships in a Hookup Culture?

This true life story from Peggy Orenstein's book, *Girls and Sex*, is a great example of how hookup culture works in this modern era. One of the stories is about a young woman whose experience highlights the repercussions of casual relationships that are built on a foundation of sex.

A. Olivia's True Life Story: The Dark Side of Hookup Culture

Olivia, a college freshman from a godly family, found herself in a world where hookup culture is the order of the day. She discovered that most students on campus don't care about connection or love; they just want to have sex with as many people as they can. To them, it's all fun and great excitement—a girl with a high body count means she's experienced, and a virgin means you are naive and missing out on the fun.

Olivia was fascinated by all this and couldn't wait to join in and experience the fun and liveliness. She wanted to be able to talk about sex with her friends and brag about her experiences. At a night party, one evening, while out with some people, she met a guy who looked very charming and was famous for being one of the hottest guys on campus.

They felt a spark of connection after a few dances, and there was an intense urge to kiss and hook up immediately—and they did. It was an amazing experience for Olivia; it felt so good and liberating to make love to a hot guy without any relationship stress.

However, after some time, she discovered that she couldn't get Jake out of her mind. She felt the need to see him again and wanted to be with him so badly. Although they had sex, their intimacy was built only on physical encounters—they had no friendship or emotional connection.

Olivia decided to take a chance and confess her growing feelings to Jake because she couldn't wait any longer. She texted him to ask if he would like to go on a date and get to know each other on a deeper level. Jake responded coldly with just one word, "Maybe," and then he ghosted her.

Olivia felt foolish for asking him such a question when he was supposed to be the one reaching out to her. She tried to understand what was happening, but she was overwhelmed with conflicting emotions and felt lost. She reached out to her roommate for advice, but the response shattered her: "That is just how it works here. You smash and move on; don't catch feelings—it ruins the fun and the excitement," her roommate said coldly.

However, Olivia still believed there was a strong connection between them and continued to try to talk to Jake for another chance to go on a date and then have sex. That seemed to work, but after a couple of hookups with Jake, she realized that Jake just didn't care about her—he just wanted to have sex and then dump her. He was not ready to be the kind of man she wanted.

One night after a party hookup, she confronted him and asked if that was the only thing he wanted and nothing more. Caught off guard, Jake laughed and said, "Look, girl, I am not in for anything serious."

For him, the sex between them was merely physical—nothing more. Jake was not ready to be the kind of man she wanted, while she, influenced by all that dopamine and oxytocin, had grown attached. In fact, it felt as though a part of him had grown on her.

Feeling heartbroken, Olivia reflected on her life and realized that hookup culture is nothing more than sex—far from what she ever wanted. She needed a man who would love and care about her, not the nonsense she had just experienced with Jake. She decided to forget about Jake, distance herself from hookup culture, and build a friendship before entering any relationship.

Olivia eventually moved on and began writing a journal about her experiences—the pain of being identified solely as a sex object in hookup culture. This helped her understand that there is love out there, but you only experience true love outside of hookup culture (in a more meaningful and wholesome setting).

Lessons from Olivia's Story

Olivia's story shows how corrupt hookup culture is and the importance of knowing your self-worth. She learns to:

1. Identify what she needs in a man: It's normal to want physical intimacy, but love—along with spiritual and emotional connection—is essential.

2. Have clear conversations: It's important to have deep discussions about what you expect from each other so that you can be on the same page.

3. Set defined boundaries: It is also essential to let the person know what you don't want in that relationship.

B. Tim Tebow's Story of Embracing Purity

Tim Tebow, a former NFL and baseball player, is a great example of living a life of purity in a society that promotes hookup culture. Infamous for his incredible athletic skills and commitment to his Christian faith and moral values, Tim abstained from premarital sex. He understood that premarital sex is against the commandments of God and knew how much damage it could cause to his life and career.

In a 2009 interview, Tebow publicly discussed how he had decided to refrain from hookup culture. He made it clear that he was looking for a partner who would love him for who he is—not because of his money or fame—and talked about the importance of having a relationship built on love and emotional connection rather than materialistic things.

Tebow's commitment to purity was met with both admiration and criticism. Especially in the professional sports world, where hookup culture is the norm, his commitment to his faith made him stand out. In 2020, Tebow married Demi-Leigh Nel-Peters, a former Miss Universe. Their relationship was built on a foundation of love, mutual respect, and emotional connection.

Tebow's story shows that you can commit to your faith and uphold purity in a corrupt society that elevates hookup culture. It also demonstrates that such discipline is both possible and rewarding. This story makes it evident that achieving purity requires self-determination and not mere wishes—it requires strong determination and a willingness to hold on to the doctrine of faith. Their relationship was built on shared values, mutual respect, and a commitment to faith. Tebow's journey underscores the possibility of maintaining personal convictions in the face of societal norms and serves as an inspiration to those who choose to prioritize purity and intentionality in their relationships.

C. Lecrae Devaughn Hopkins (Lecrae): Another Life of Purity

Lecrae is a talented and Grammy Award-winning rapper and renowned Christian whose talents did not stop him from committing to the Christian faith in a hookup-oriented industry. His strength to overcome temptations and remain unstained is astonishing.

His Early Lifestyle

Lecrae grew up in an unhealthy environment that introduced him to smoking, drugs, and violence. In his early life, he made some bad decisions and found himself in casual relationships that were toxic and draining. However, everything changed when he found Jesus; he discovered that what he had been doing was not the way of the Lord. He gave his life to Christ and started working toward achieving a great career in life.

He realized that there is love and joy in living a life of purity and separating oneself from casual relationships. His new life stood in contrast to the hookup culture that has overtaken the hip hop and entertainment industry, where sexual wildness is paramount.

He married Darragh Moore, and their marriage was built on trust, faith, and love. Lecrae and Darragh did not have a random, worldly relationship; they intended to get married and focused on building friendship, as well as spiritual and emotional connections, before any physical encounter. Their relationship is evidence that it's rewarding to choose love over just a casual relationship.

The Impact of Purity on His Career

Despite the difficulties and challenges he faced in refraining from the negative norms of the entertainment industry, Lecrae did not become weary. He remained steadfast in his faith and his commitment to living a life that pleases God.

He openly declared his Christian faith and his decision to set himself apart, making him a role model for many people around the world, including his fans. Lecrae not only declared his faith but also used his social media platforms to talk about God's love for mankind.

Despite the pressure to conform to the norms of the entertainment industry, Lecrae remained firm in his beliefs. His openness about his faith and commitment to purity has not only set him apart but has also made him a role model.

Lecrae has used his platform to advocate for living authentically, making decisions that align with one's faith, and rejecting the superficial standards of fame and fortune. His lifestyle is a living testimony to how God empowers His children in a hookup-oriented industry to overcome temptations. He has given us the power to overcome sin. By choosing the narrow path that leads to heaven, Lecrae has become a beacon of hope for those who are weary of following the path of righteousness in relationships. Lecrae was given fame as well as temptations—evidence that you have the power to choose moral values and purity even when society and everything else tell you otherwise.

Relationships that have God at the center will always prevail, no matter the difficulties they face in their journey. You need to have someone you can always trust in your corner. God is the one who will never disappoint you. He says that He has a plan for you which is not evil and will lead you to a fulfilling end. He has many people He can bring into your journey to help make it smoother because they have walked the path before. Regardless of your childhood—whether good or bad—God will always come through for you if you allow Him to guide you. The trauma of the past, whether from your upbringing or from your past dating experiences, cannot stop His plan. All you need to do is allow Him to take the lead, and when He nudges your instinct to act—even if only for a millisecond or microsecond—act accordingly, and you will not regret it.

CHAPTER NINE

DEALING WITH PAST MISTAKES – HOW TO MOVE FORWARD WITH GRACE

"Master, this woman was taken in adultery, in the very act. Now Moses in the law commanded us that such should be stoned; but what say you?" This they said, tempting Him, that they might have a basis to accuse Him. But Jesus stooped down, and with His finger wrote on the ground, as though He heard them not. When they continued questioning Him, He lifted Himself up and said to them, "He that is without sin among you, let him first cast a stone at her." And again He stooped down and wrote on the ground. Then those who heard were convicted by their own conscience and went out one by one, beginning with the eldest, even unto the last; and Jesus was left alone with the woman standing in the midst. When Jesus lifted Himself up and saw no one but the woman, He said to her, "Woman, where are those your accusers? Has no man condemned you?" She replied, "No man, Lord." And Jesus said to her, "Neither do I condemn you; go, and sin no more." (John 8:4–11)

One of the best things about being a child of God is that He does not hold our mistakes against us. In fact, unlike other religions where people are required to pay for their sins with offerings, sacrifices, or punishments, we as children of God have an advocate who sits at the right hand of the Father, interceding for us. This is why God Himself offered Jesus as the ultimate sacrifice—once and for all—to help us when we fall.

From the days of Adam and Eve, God has seen our mistakes and impurities and has been establishing ways to draw man back to Himself. His love for us is so profound and unshakable that when we fall, He does not see failure; He sees an opportunity to show us what His mercy, love, and abundant grace feel like. When we sin or grieve Him, He patiently waits for our repentance and for us to ask for His mercy. Thus, you do not fail God on the day you make a drastic mistake; you fail God the day you turn your heart away from Him. You fail His love the day you fail to run back to Him. You fail yourself the day you ignore the blood that is readily available at the cross to wash you clean.

The Bible calls this kind of unrepentant heart "the heart of stone." Ezekiel 36:26–27 says, "And I will give you a new heart, and a new spirit I will put within you. And I will remove the heart of stone from your flesh and give you a heart of flesh. And I will put my Spirit within you and cause you to walk in my statutes and be careful to obey my rules."

Satan understands how easy it is to embrace repentance; that is why he poisons your mind and hardens your heart against opening up to the Spirit of God. If only people ran back to God at the slightest falter, the devil would have no one to torment or torture with chronic sin. This is why the Bible also warns us to guard our hearts with all diligence, because out of it are the issues of life.

How Should We Handle Mistakes?

Each and every one of us has, at least once, reached a point where we did things we never planned or intended to do. Somehow, we find ourselves in places we vowed we'd never be, doing things we claimed could never be us. These experiences form the bank of mistakes from which we learn. They are like scars, and our scars tell the story of God's grace in our lives, of our strength, and of times when we had every reason to give up—but He held us in faith and hope in CHRIST.

Everybody makes mistakes, though in different ways and degrees. Your mistakes might seem more severe or less significant, but you are not the first to have erred. Mistakes provide valuable experience, and that experience teaches you important lessons. You need to learn from your mistakes so you don't repeat them. You need to understand the emotional trauma that can accompany casual sex and learn from it. If you have experienced health issues as a result of poor relationships, you don't need anyone else to explain the lesson to you. And if you do not learn from your mistakes, you will continue to repeat them until you finally do.

I know a story about a barber who, after finishing his apprenticeship, launched a new barber salon in a promising, bustling environment. It wasn't long before he began to get customers; sadly, his very first customer was disappointed with the haircut. The client's hairline was uneven and crooked—in fact, it was terrible! However, after a few explanations and apologies, he got paid and was content with the outcome.

Another client walked in the following day, and the same mistake repeated itself. It was awful. The customer complained, but this time he didn't care; after all, he had been paid before the service was rendered.

More customers experienced the same issue, and soon he became well known for being terribly bad at his job. He eventually decided to go back for a brush-up and correct his flaws, but before he could fix his mistakes, he had already lost many customers. After several incidents with clients, he had to relocate from that environment completely. He started over elsewhere and eventually became an excellent barber after learning from his mistakes, though he could never undo the errors of his past.

What point are we trying to make? Even the great cobbler of today once mended shoes incorrectly, and the popular barber you know was once prone to giving bad haircuts. Yet, they all learned from their mistakes and became the finest versions of themselves.

Mistakes shape who we are, especially when we learn the lessons from them. It's okay to err, but whether you remain stuck in that mess or move forward determines if your past will mar you or make you. God wants us to move forward in the life He has given us, and being stuck is never part of His will. These mistakes have shaped us in ways that words cannot fully describe. They are our journey, our scars, our lessons to learn, and our stories to tell.

You may ask yourself, "Did that thing have to happen? Why wasn't I warned that this seemingly harmless friendship would be the reason I get raped? Why didn't I know that talking to this person would change me?" You didn't know what to do because you are human, and making mistakes is common; however, the steps you take from then on can make a world of difference. You can either sink into self-pity and cry yourself into a stupor over what has already happened, or you can clean yourself up, identify the steps you missed, and move on. We cannot ignore the fact that we might have been warned—by our conscience or by others—but we chose to look the other way because we were already emotionally invested in people who, unbeknownst to us, would eventually betray us. Be that as it may, move on. Count your losses, work on recovery and self-discovery, and strive to move on completely.

If only people knew where certain paths would lead, they might never have embarked on some of the journeys we did.

Unfortunately, if you do not recognize the voice of the Holy Spirit because you do not yet have a relationship with God, you may be clueless about the precise direction of His perfect will for your life. There are many ways, but there is also a path that guarantees a fulfilled life here on earth and an eternal home in heaven. Wandering aimlessly and leaving the trajectory of your life to chance is not an option. Be intentional, therefore, about the direction you want your life to take by simply making your choice in His Word.

At the end of the day, we have all experienced moments when our morals or principles fail us, and we stumble. Some people overcome mistakes easily, but for others, the weight of their actions crushes them. Shame begins to creep in, suffocating you; you start to believe that your future is completely lost, feeling bleak and unworthy of healing, and, worst of all, ashamed to face God.

It is in these moments of brokenness and torment that the grace of God appears as a lifeline. At that moment, you realize that God's grace is not merely a concept but your only hope. You tell yourself that you've messed up, yet God's grace reminds you that where your strength failed, His grace made you stronger. You may think you're too filthy to approach the throne of God, but His grace reminds you that if righteousness were all that mattered, He would never have needed to die. You might even think that God hates you at your worst, but that is precisely when His love reaches out to you. Paul was on his way to persecute Christians when grace found him. The adulterous woman was caught red-handed when Jesus advocated for her. Your mistakes do not define you! I repeat: your mistakes are nothing compared to the future God has in store for you. That is the beauty of God's grace—it does not require your perfection; rather, it meets you right in the midst of your mess! It does not instruct you to simply shower and appear clean; instead, it invites you to begin again—to start anew, right where you are.

The inability to clean out the closet and keep moving forward leads to the recurring failures some people experience. The devil does not want you to rise and move forward. If you allow him, he wants to control your mind, gate-keep your thought process, and keep you depressed over the mistakes of your past. However, God's plan is for you to take charge, dispel the enemy's lies, and move on to victory—because victory is only possible when you have conquered it in your mind.

The True Nature of Regret and Learning to Forgive Yourself

Regret moves silently, creeping upon you when you're alone or striking you heavily when you least expect it. Sometimes, all it takes is the mention of a name to trigger that heaviness. Other times, you see people living the life you always dreamed of and regret the choices you made that ruined that life for you. It comes upon you, leaving you burdened with a weight that no one else can alleviate—a weight only you can feel.

The thing about regret is that it is normal to feel it, but it is not meant to be your prison. Instead, it should serve as your teacher—a painful motivator, guiding you toward where you are meant to be and what you are meant to do. It can be your guide, not your chains.

Some people say things like, "I don't care if everyone forgives me; I will never forgive myself." For such people, it is a form of self-atonement—a way to pay for their mistakes. Self-condemnation only keeps you stuck in your past; it does not heal you.

When Jesus addressed the woman caught in adultery, He did not tell her, "I forgive you, but you should not forget what you did. You need to keep beating yourself up for a while to make up for this." Instead, He said, "Go and sin no more." In that moment, He set her free—not only from her sin but also from the shame that her sin had brought upon her. He granted her permission to move on with grace, just as He gives you permission to continue your life with His grace. This does not excuse your mistake; rather, it acknowledges that you are only human and that your worth is not tied to your past.

How to Start Afresh

To start over after faltering, you need to adjust your perspective on life. You cannot erase the past, but you should ask yourself these questions:

1. Why did this happen?

2. What am I supposed to learn from it?

3. How do I ensure this mistake does not affect my future?

Allow what has happened to motivate you to make better decisions for yourself. Think of your life as a book; one sad page does not define the entire story. With every fresh page you turn, you have the opportunity to add fulfilling narratives to your story. You might ask yourself, "How do I do this? I don't know where to start." Just begin anywhere, and allow the grace of God to transform you.

The Role of Our Environment

It is almost impossible for healing to occur in isolation, so you must be very selective about the people with whom you spend time during this phase. Associating with people who are comfortable with sin or premarital sex is the fastest way to find yourself engaging in the very behavior you regret. However, surrounding yourself with people who remind you of God's truth, who encourage and support your journey, makes all the difference. Sometimes, it can be just one friend, a counselor, or a small group of like-minded individuals; having someone who understands your struggles and celebrates your victories is priceless.

However, it is perfectly acceptable to keep to yourself if those around you cannot be trusted to support you in the right way. The last thing you need is people spreading gossip or judging you when you are struggling to find your way back to the right path.

Lies That Wrong Associates Will Tell You When You're Trying to Start Over

Starting afresh is not easy—especially if you were deeply entrenched in sin. In fact, it is one of the bravest decisions you can make, but there will be people who mock or ridicule your choice. They will, both consciously and unconsciously, try to undermine your progress by saying things that make you doubt yourself or rekindle your shame. The most painful aspect is that these lies often come from friends, family, acquaintances, or even trusted individuals. The first step to dispelling these lies is to recognize them for what they are: lies.

1. **"Changing is impossible; it's just who you are."**

   People will bring up your past mistakes and try to convince you that you can never escape that cycle of sin and carelessness. They will say that people do not truly change, or claim that you've always been that person. The truth is, not only is change possible, but it is also essential for pursuing your purpose. Those who say otherwise know nothing about human growth or the transformative power of God's grace and forgiveness. Consider Paul, who was on his way to persecute Christians but ended up preaching salvation to the lost (Acts 9). Leave your past behind and focus on the choices you make moving forward. Old things have passed away, and all things have become new (2 Corinthians 5:17).

2. **"Nobody forgets what you did; you will always be judged by your actions."**

   People will tell you that nothing you do can change their perception of you—that is their burden to bear. They might say, "No one can believe you are different now," or "I can never take you seriously." Ultimately, that is their business because they have chosen to dwell on your past. They will prey on your desire for public acceptance and your fear of criticism. Remember, the fear of man is a snare, but trust in the Lord is safe (Proverbs 29:25). It is true that the world takes time to recognize change, but over time, your consistent attitude and actions will speak louder than any past mistake.

3. **"You can't start over now; it's too late for that."**

Every new day is a fresh opportunity to be the person you want to be. There is no timeline for starting over or living a new, positive life. Even Moses was 80 when God called him to lead the Israelites out of Egypt, and Sarah was 90 when she bore Isaac. It is never too late for God to do something good with your life; it is never too late for you to start over. In Joel 2:25, God promises, "I will restore to you all the years that the locust has eaten." He does not need you to be perfect; broken things become blessed when you allow God to mend them.

4. **"You'll never find anything better than this relationship."**

People often try to make you feel that they are the best thing you will ever have when you decide to make drastic, positive decisions for yourself—such as walking away from them. A big-time flirt or sex addict might say things like, "Oh, you think anyone else will love you? No one else will be with someone like you; you should be grateful I even came your way." All of this is designed to undermine your self-worth by convincing you that they are irreplaceable. At this point, you need to listen to your heart and to what the Spirit of God is saying. Study the Word of God and boldly proclaim that you are a chosen generation—a royal priesthood called to declare the praises of Him who has called you (1 Peter 2:9). This lie is a cheap tactic designed to leave you questioning your decisions; if you are not careful, you will be ensnared in the belief that no one else will love you for your values and principles.

5. **"Your new choices can't last for long; you will revert back faster than you think."**

It is true that starting on a new course can be challenging, especially after old patterns have been established. The lie the devil will try to instill in your mind is: "You already failed your morals and beliefs in the past; what makes you think you can do it differently this time?" This lie seeks to diminish your sincerity and repentance, undermining the growth, change, and power of the Holy Spirit working within you to bring out the best in you.

Isaiah 43:18–19 says, "Forget the former things; do not dwell on the past. See, I am doing a new thing! Now it springs up; do you not perceive it? I am making a way in the wilderness and rivers in the deserts."

You must understand that the promises of God are clear and true. *He loves you. He has forgiven you. Your past does not disqualify you from his love. You are a changed person. It is still early enough to start over.*

Change doesn't happen overnight; it is not magic. You will face challenges, but with a renewed mind—as the scripture assures us that there is no condemnation for those in Christ—your defenses against old habits will be strengthened.

1 Peter 2:15

"For so is the will of God, that with well-doing you may put to silence the ignorance of foolish men."

Ensure you celebrate every tiny victory, such as simply turning down a date with the wrong person or choosing to spend time studying the Word of God rather than watching unhealthy television programs.

CHAPTER TEN

PRACTICAL HABITS TO ACHIEVE SUCCESS IN SEXUAL PURITY (WISDOM FOR DAILY LIVING)

A. Understanding How Triggers Work to Negatively Control Your Actions

Triggers can be described as internal or external factors that drive your thoughts, actions, or desires toward certain acts you wish to avoid. These factors try to get your attention—even against your will—through captivating messages, seductive content, images, cues, and trends that pull out parts of us we struggle to bury, causing our struggle for purity to become a battlefield.

One thing we need to understand is that the path to purity is not just about avoiding traps and temptations; rather, it's more about living a life that honors God and everything He represents through you (righteousness, peace, love, patience, etc.). To be successful in this journey, it is important to identify those factors that are your major temptations or triggers and develop realistic habits that serve as a defense and reinforce your commitment to living a life of purity.

Triggers Commonly Found Around Us

1. **Social Media and Visual Media**

Social media videos, TV programs, or movies with normalized explicit scenes can stir up your bodily longings for premarital sex. A romantic TV show might seem harmless and swoon-worthy anytime, any day, but it unconsciously sows seeds of sexual desire in your mind until you eventually find yourself in bed with the opposite sex, fulfilling those lustful desires.

2. Social Gatherings

Gatherings such as crazy parties with smokers and alcoholic enthusiasm often lead to intense sexual energy and impulsive sexual intercourse. At first, it seems harmless to go to that party because your friend or course-mate invited you, but when alcohol-driven conversations and steamy games begin to test your boundaries—with nowhere to escape or with many people cheering you on—you fall.

3. Idleness and Lack of Spiritual Focus

Staying idle and not meditating on the word of God when you find yourself alone and less busy sometimes gives you room to indulge in filthy memories, thoughts, or imaginations. To worsen this, you might begin to randomly scroll through your phone until you encounter media content that causes you to click and continue until you find yourself sex-chatting, masturbating, or even dressing up to have casual sex with someone you shouldn't be involved with.

4. Reminders of Past Immorality

Meeting up with people with whom you have an immoral history or going to places associated with past sexual experiences has a way of reigniting old flames and ultimately causing you to repeat habits you're not proud of. For instance, if you broke up with someone who does not encourage your stand for sexual purity, you have no business keeping them on your social media or storing their memories on your phone. They should be blocked, deleted, and forgotten if you intend to move on for good.

There are other common triggers that you can naturally identify in your environment. Do well to list them out, recognizing that they have the potential to cause you to falter or fall in your journey.

How to Identify What Triggers You Sexually

I. Study and observe the patterns. At what point does your temptation become consuming? When do you usually feel the most tempted?

II. Reflect on loopholes and activities that played out in those patterns. What would you say caused you to feel so heated up? What led to that?

III. Take notes and journal your activities and emotions during these moments so as to keep track of these recurring patterns and know them for what they are.

Steps to Adhere to in Order To Neutralize Things that Trigger You

✓ Take charge of your environment

This includes both your physical and digital spaces. Do away with magazines, books, tapes, and anything that feeds your temptations. Also, filter and free your devices of certain triggers by unfollowing or blocking accounts that promote explicit content and replacing them with faith-based podcasts, personalities, and songs.

✓ Set clear boundaries

Be intentional about the boundaries you set to protect your mind from these traps by limiting or not engaging in conversations geared toward flirtation or immorality. Also, avoid meeting up with the opposite gender in private settings because this could be a trap you are not even aware of. Additionally, let your boundaries regarding physical touch be known through your actions or words.

If someone doesn't keep their hands to themselves or touches your body at the slightest opportunity, communicate this boundary clearly because those touches influence your mind sooner or later.

✓ Control your thoughts

Whenever wandering thoughts arise in your mind, snap out of them as quickly as possible and do not engage with them. Ask the Holy Spirit to fill your mind with thoughts worthy of His presence. Temptations are born in the mind, and it is your responsibility to filter the things you allow in your thoughts. Finally, brethren, whatsoever things are true, whatsoever things are honest, whatsoever things are just, whatsoever things are pure, whatsoever things are lovely, whatsoever things are of good report; if there be any virtue, and if there be any praise, think on these things.

✓ Choose your company wisely

You can't try to avoid a certain behavior while continuing to hang around people who practice what you wish to avoid. Surround yourself with people who are on the same path as you, and your journey will be easier. Joining active Christian communities can also keep you focused by keeping you engaged in kingdom projects and feeding your soul with the right activities. 1 Corinthians 15:33 warns, "Do not be misled: 'Bad company corrupts good character.'" Be intentional about who you allow into your inner circle.

B. How to Build a Living Pattern Which Supports Your Journey

In part A of this chapter, we discussed triggers and how they work to make people derail. However, you should understand that knowing your triggers and staying away from them is only a fragment of the whole picture. We need to thrive, and to thrive, your old living habits must be replaced with new choices and habits that fuel your path to absolute righteousness.

Choosing a path of sexual purity is an intentional choice you make daily as you stay disciplined and depend on God's grace; it is not a one-off subscription that you just take and leave. Every day, we wake up to various distractions, and remaining in purity—through our actions, thoughts, and relationships—demands practical daily habits that we abide by.

Consider these habits as a spiritual toolbox used to keep you on the right track, equipping you to lead a spiritually balanced life in faith. Here are practical strategies to help you stay committed to purity, one day at a time. Let's explore a few of them:

1. **Begin with a clear and sincere goal**

   Some people say things to appear holy or for show; however, in their minds, they are practicing self-deceit because they can't fool God. Before you begin this journey, ask yourself: Am I honest about this decision? Having learned all that I now understand about sexual immorality and its baggage, do I want to abstain from sexual immorality and only have sex within the boundaries of marriage? If yes, you're on the right track. Now ask yourself again: What does purity mean to me? Do I need to protect my mind from filthy thoughts? What boundaries do I need to put in place when dealing with relationships? How should I react when I am tempted?

   Write down your practical and realistic responses to these questions. These reflections are essential because it is important to know where your journey is headed even before you embark on it. Clarifying your vision will keep you on track, focused, and rooted in that course. Even the Bible has clearly stated, "Where there is no vision, the people perish."

2. **Let your daily routine be infused with faith**

    o   Make sure that you do not begin any day without prayer and meditation on Scripture. When you put God first every day, you condition your mind to be alert against the arrows of the enemy.

    o   Never go to bed without absolute gratitude to God, thankful for how His grace sustained you through the day despite the challenges you faced. Say a prayer of gratitude before you retire to bed and meditate on His promises for you.

3. **Work toward your dreams and purpose and put in the hard work required to achieve your targets**

    o   Staying focused on meaningful objectives keeps you occupied with worthy pursuits, rather than spending your time and resources chasing after immorality.

    o   If you don't have any key activity going on at the moment, volunteering at an organization that aligns with your passion is also a good way to start.

4. **Buy a journal and document your journey**

    This is a life-changing approach for staying accountable and reflecting on your progress. Journaling is a tool that helps you analyze your thoughts, filter them, identify your triggers, and track your entire journey.

    o   Write down your challenges and your victories.

    o   Reflect on the temptations from which God has delivered you and recognize His strength in your life.

    o   Note your struggles or setbacks and continue asking God for the grace to deal with them successfully. For example, you could write about "situations that tested my resolution today and how I will respond if those things occur again." In summary, journaling teaches you to be honest with yourself and creates a safe space for sincere tracking of your journey.

5. **Take your physical, emotional, and mental health seriously.** A healthy mind and body provide fertile ground for wise choices and decisions.

    o   Engage in daily exercise to manage fatigue and build strength.

    o   If you have unresolved emotional burdens or trauma, seek counseling to help you overcome any emotional challenges that may slow you down if ignored.

6. **Be accountable even in the little things so that you won't struggle when you eventually encounter bigger issues.**

    o   Discussions on topics of interest can serve as a lamp that prepares you for what lies ahead. This can be with a mentor or a trusted friend/confidant.

    o   Establish a routine for discussing challenges, progress, and successes. James 5:16 encourages, "Confess your sins to one another and pray for one another, that you may be healed." Staying accountable to the right partner provides strength and encouragement.

7. **Always remember that God's grace is sufficient when you make mistakes and ask for His mercy as often as you stumble.**

    o   Go before Him at any point you feel lost, stuck, or weary. He will lighten your burden.

o   Reflect on your mistakes and be determined not to fall into such temptation in the future.

o   Meditate on Romans 8:1: "There is now no condemnation for those who are in Christ Jesus." Remember that a mistake isn't a sign of failure but a reminder that you're human and need the grace of God at every point in your life to succeed.

C. Daily Affirmations for a Life of Sexual Purity

Maintaining a commitment to purity is much like the first step of any great journey. Walking the fine line between personal hardships, social expectations, and moments of weakness is not always simple.

Here's the thing, though: your thoughts have great power. The words you say to yourself have the power to influence your attitude, fortify your determination, and direct your behavior.

Daily affirmations serve as anchors for your heart and mind, as statements of your ideals, and as reminders of your mission. They are more than just words—they provide protection from negativity and uncertainty, as well as encouragement when things seem unclear.

By repeating these affirmations to yourself every day, you will be reminded of your value, your resilience, and your capacity to live a life filled with dignity, self-respect, and purpose.

Progress, not flawlessness, is the focus of these affirmations. They are resources to help you refocus, maintain your composure, and confidently move toward your objectives. Whether you're just beginning your journey or you're looking for the willpower to keep going, let these affirmations inspire you. You can certainly live out what you believe in with courage and grace, and you are not alone.

Center your mind, take a deep breath, and confidently say these affirmations. Let them be your daily reminder that purity is about embracing clarity, strength, and a purposeful future rather than merely the things you avoid.

Empowering Daily Affirmations for Purity

1. "My actions honor my value at every point because I am wonderfully and fearfully made."

   This means my soul, my body, and my heart are sacred, and I always treat them with dignity and respect.

2. "The strength of God in me overwhelms and overpowers the temptations I encounter daily."

   Hence, I have been given all it takes to thrive in purity and faith.

3. "I am not in any way bound to my past. The grace of God has redeemed and renewed me, and I stand right with God."

   Going forward, I have the chance to embrace a new life of purpose and fulfillment on a daily basis.

4. "My purity aligns with the mind-blowing future God has laid out for me, and I choose it with ease."

   The decisions I make represent the version of me that exists in my future.

5. "The wisdom of God guards my heart because it is the wellspring of life."

   I allow only things that nourish my body and soul to come in.

6. "I find only the God kind of love that cherishes, honors, and protects me."

   I am not made to settle for the selfish lust that comes from the world.

7. "I find grace to turn my back on everything that opposes my principles and walk with God."

And by doing this, my joy and satisfaction with God are protected.

8. "I find happiness in living a life of abstinence, as it represents my love for God and my value for myself."

Purity is a joyful decision and act of worship.

9. "I have absolute trust in God, and I know He is putting things together to fulfill every desire of my heart in His perfect time."

I know that God's plan for me is worth every bit of patience and sacrifice I make today.

10. "My path is victorious, and my feet shall not slide."

I am clothed in victory and strength, and I have everything I need to remain triumphant.

11. "The Holy Spirit in me is a priceless gift of God."

My actions do not grieve Him; He finds expression through me.

12. "There is no temptation I meet that I am not armored against."

As a child of God, nothing takes me by surprise, and my victory over temptations is assured.

13. "My thoughts are pure; my mind is guarded with truth and decency."

My mind is not a fertile ground for impurities or distractions.

14. "My future is not determined by any mistake from the past, but by the promises of God."

I am therefore not condemned by the things that are behind me because I press forward toward the mark of Christ.

Feel free to write as many affirmations as resonate with your struggle, as the Holy Spirit will guide you. Take time to declare them daily until they melt into your subconscious and become your reality.

To lead a life of sexual cleanliness in our world today is not an easy feat, but it can become one of the most profitable paths you ever embark on. When you work toward incorporating these patterns into your daily living, you set yourself up for a successful journey. When you struggle, don't forget that it's not a journey of perfection but one of learning and hard work, of reliance on God's grace. Each situation you find yourself in is a chance to exercise your muscles of purity, to grow in faith, and to live in the glory of a godly, devoted life.

CONCLUSION

THE BOLD CHOICE OF PURITY – A LIFE OF STRENGTH AND PURPOSE

Your decision to lead a pure life has the capacity to transform not only your own life but also the lives of people in your immediate surroundings. You are establishing a new benchmark, defying social norms, and leaving a legacy of determination and faith.

Consider the ramifications of your choice—how your bravery can encourage others to rise above the chaos and live a meaningful life. "Blessed are the pure in heart, for they shall see God," said Jesus Himself (Matthew 5:8). This is about living in the fullness of God's presence and blessings, rather than simply about abiding by the laws. You are aligning yourself with His plan when you choose purity, and that plan is always superior to everything else. If you have previously suffered or made decisions you later regret, know that your journey is not yet done.

Purity is a daily choice, and God's grace is always there to support you in making a fresh start. It's never too late to start over, which is the wonderful thing about this experience.

In other words, don't fret. Accept God's boundless grace and let go of your shame. He is aware of your hardships, sees your heart, and rejoices in each step you take in His direction.

Now is your time—a chance to rise above all the noise, maintain your moral principles, and enjoy the remarkable life that purity brings.

It won't always be easy, and the most wonderful things in life are rarely easy. When doubts start to creep in, keep in mind that you are worth the wait. It's worth the sacrifice for your future. Your goal is worth the struggle.

Allow this choice to serve as a statement to the world and to yourself: I am resilient. I am deserving. I'm after the bigger picture. And while you stick to this path, be proud that you are choosing power, freedom, and a life of lasting significance rather than just purity. Therefore, move forward with confidence. Be bold in every aspect of your life. Tell your story to inspire others and remember that each time you choose sexual purity, you are simultaneously making the decision to live a life that represents the unfathomable love and purpose of your Creator. And guess what? Your treasures are still much. The best is on its way.

ABOUT THE AUTHOR

Stephen Owolabi is a seasoned Bible teacher and author with extensive experience in youth ministry and mentoring the next generation. His passion for empowering others through biblical truths is evident in his writings and teachings.

Stephen has authored several impactful books, including Communion on the Altar, Language Successful People Speak, and In Pursuit of Destiny. Each of his works reflects his commitment to inspiring purposeful living through faith and wisdom.

He is the President of SoundMind World Inc., an outreach ministry based in Indianapolis, USA, dedicated to spreading God's Word and equipping individuals for spiritual growth and success.

Made in the USA
Monee, IL
18 May 2025

17681019R00066